Tom,

If I was [illegible] .... ,
I would have had this book
published within 3 months
(instead of 1 year!).

Thanks for your help and
support while I was at
Homesteaders!

MW01612010

Tom

What Others Are Saying About This Book

"All humans benefit by reconnecting to nature, even in settings where we believe there is little opportunity. In "Learning from a Duck", Tom has borrowed nature's lessons and found relevant metaphors that can help guide, inspire, and teach the business world some of the time-tested wisdom that Life has honed over millennia. This perspective might just change how you think about nature, and your business."
Dayna Baumeister, PhD,
Co founder Biomimicry Guild

"A management book with a wealth of pictures speaks to the heart and the brain, exactly what is needed to move our economy towards sustainability."
Gunter Pauli
Founder, Zero Emissions Research & Initiatives

"Humanity emerged from the natural world. Personal interactions, group dynamics, universal Human values, and global commerce all derive from the ancient laws and relationships of nature. And yet far too many people have forgotten or never learned this fundamental, inescapable fact of life. Tom's book can help us all get back in touch with that which sustains us and we urgently need to embrace these timeless lessons."
Ted Townsend
Founder, Great Ape Trust

"There was a time when humans learned many lessons from nature. That was before TV, computers, and the internet, but those lessons are still available. If now, in the 21st century with all the email, Facebooks, Twitters, and so on, you doubt that there's anything nature can possibly teach you about business, then read this book. Tom Porter has, in effect, created a new piece of wisdom literature."
James A. Autry
Author, The Servant Leader and Looking Around for God

"Everything is part of the natural world, and not only is it not nice to try to fool Mother Nature, in the end, it is impossible. Nature will always win. Tom Porter has pointed to the primal insight that understanding natural forces are as relevant in the boardroom as they are in the woods, and has done so with wit, wisdom, and delight."
Robert Fritz
Author, The Path of Least Resistance for Managers

"Refreshing, engaging, humane, thought-provoking; don't read this one too fast."
Stephen Kaplan & Rachel Kaplan, Professors, University of Michigan
Environment and Behavior School of Natural Resources and Environment

"In our modern lives the opportunity to explore ourselves through nature has become increasingly scarce. However our need for self-reflection and the type of renewal which nature provides is more important than ever. Tom Porter's latest book provides us with a collection of mini-expeditions that are as energizing as they are insightful, and make the perfect companion for those moments at the office when the door is just a bit too far away."
Charlie Wittmack
Adventurer, Attorney, Speaker
(Probably best known for climbing Mount Everest in 2003)

"The natural world is beautiful to behold. Within its beauty, there is a wealth of insight to explore and hold within each of us. Tom captures these rich wisdoms, then connects them to business, in all its complexity and pure simplicity. This is not a text as much it is a collection of poems to the business leader, through the eyes of a caring thinker."
Peter Gerritsen
President, TAAN (Transworld Advertising Agency Network)

"In stillness, our ancestors, gleaned the profound lessons of nature, brought them back to their communities, told stories about what they had learned and applied the lessons to their daily lives. Tom Porter is our modern day emissary, reminding us of the wisdom that nature freely offers, if we are willing to listen. This book is a can't-do-without, esthetically pleasing, very practical, well-researched guide to conscious business practices."
Ann Romberg and Lynn Baskfield, Principals
Wisdom Horse Coaching, LLC

"Tom's uncanny gift to see and hear what others often miss served him well in his successful business career. Now, in his new book, he shares how each of us can sharpen our senses and glean practical life and business lessons by being a better student of the world around us…you'll never see things quite the same. A fascinating read!"
Graham J. Cook, President & CEO
Homesteaders Life Company

"Tom Porter, in his book, "Learning from a Duck" has delivered sophisticated nature lessons that provide us with unique insight about nature and important lessons for running a business. If green is the color of this millennium, then the successful business of our time will be green as well, less management by cliché more in the simple interdependent and ethical way that nature teaches us."
Rick McMaster, Executive Director
North Idaho Health Network

All I Need To Know About Business I Learned From A Duck

Business Lessons From Nature

Tom Porter

dog ear
PUBLISHING

Dog Ear Publishing, Indianapolis, Indiana

ISBN: 978-160844-301-7
Library of Congress Control Number: Applied for

Cover and text design by Craig LeClere

To my wife, Susan,
who has taught me more
than she will ever know.

To my children Brandon, Marshall and Logan,
who molded me into a decent father.

And to Jake, who showed me that
we have much to learn from nature.

Acknowledgements

I cannot take credit for creating the contents of this book because it is the result of my interactions and studies with all the individuals I am about to list, and many others. The list is incomplete because it does not include all of the clients, colleagues, friends, teachers and associates that have helped me over the years. So if you do not find your name on this page please know that on some level you helped shape this book, and I deeply appreciate your contribution.

First, to Craig LeClere who designed the front cover and inside spreads of this book, and who I had the honor of working with for 21 ½ years at Porter & Associates. I express deep appreciation for your creativity and willingness to take a chance with me, once again. I wanted to create something unique in the business book category – a book that would fully engage readers visually and emotionally through their hearts, and once again your creativity and execution were incredible.

To Jim Stafford and Abe Goldstien, my former colleagues and shareholders at Porter & Associates I appreciate all that you did to help grow the agency and for putting up with me as I experimented with many of the concepts provided in this book.

To my friends who encouraged me throughout this process: Rick & Paula McMaster, Mike & Linda Thies, Steve & Bev Stone, Ted Townsend, Pat Lofthouse, Drew McLellan, Toni Jacobson, Elizabeth Saunders, Larry Crowell, Marsha Hines, Katy Fletcher, Shirley Poertner, Wayne Marshall and everyone at Common Thread.

I am also grateful to Michael Gerber, Keith Raniere, Nancy Saltzman, Almut & Rhett Hatfield, Angela Farmer & Victor van Kooten, Carol Gurney and Deb Sheppard for providing me with new perspectives and unique experiences that helped shape my current world-view.

I also thank Graham Cook for furnishing me with the extraordinary opportunity of experiencing corporate life as an employee … not the owner. And to Tim Hayes, who has taught me as much as I hope I have taught him in our mentoring sessions.

CONTENTS

Introduction

Why I wrote this book

Do you remember the 1976 satirical movie Network? The film is about a fictional television network and its faltering audience ratings. One of the most famous scenes is where Howard Beale (Peter Finch, who plays a news anchor) has been fired because of low ratings. He's been provided with an opportunity to make a dignified exit from the UBS Evening News, but instead Beale rants about how life isn't fair and screams at the top of his lungs, "I'm mad as hell and I'm not going to take this anymore!"

I consider myself to be a reasonably evolved person, so I'm somewhat embarrassed to admit that like Beale, upon reading recent accounts of how some of the top executives in America's largest corporations personally financially gained by stripping and destroying the value of their companies, I lost my cool and wanted to shout out, "Those sleazy bastards should be tar and feathered!"

Instead, I sat down at my desk and starting writing this book.

Erosion of business ethics

Sitting at my computer I considered whether business ethics had actually plummeted to new lows, or whether I was merely blowing the current situation out of proportion. After all, corruption in business isn't anything new. So what was it about the current reports of mismanagement and corporate greed that bothered me so much?

In gathering my thoughts I reflected upon my 22 years as a small business owner, my 3 ½ years as an officer of a life insurance company, and my current gig as a marketing consultant and author. I determined that in business, as in life, everything is an exchange. Just as the leaves in trees provide the air we breathe with oxygen in exchange for the carbon dioxide it absorbs, employees exchange their time, knowledge and effort for salaries and benefits, and for the feeling they receive from participating in something bigger than they could create on their own.

Unfortunately in today's economy, too many employees are being forced to trade time they could be spending interacting and relaxing with family and friends for conducting business after hours and on weekends because their employer tightened budgets and is "doing more with less". Even more disturbing is that more and more employees and top executives are exchanging their ethics for the security of a paycheck and associated healthcare benefits. Why? Primarily because the average American today is in hock up to his or her eyeballs with credit card balances and mortgage payments that are so burdensome, employees and top executives can't afford to lose their job ... so they look the other way when they witness white collar crime and other breaches of ethics.

On top of all that, there is unprecedented pressure on business leaders in major corporations to produce profits and ever increasing returns on investments. This combined with workers who are overextended financially, has contributed to a Perfect Storm of unethical business practices that eventually caused the economic, financial and moral collapse of the century.

Even owners and managers of small to medium-sized businesses are beginning to toss aside longstanding personal and corporate values. Loyalty to long-time employees, commitment to training and mentoring of new employees and exceeding customer's expectations has been sacrificed to generate short-term profitability. All of which serves to fuel fear-based management practices, distrust between management and employees, and low levels of job satisfaction.

While there is no way to prove it, I feel that ethical behavior in business today has hit an all-time low. Some say the way out is more government intervention, which in my opinion is like going from the frying pan into the fire. I also feel that the problem cannot be solved by using the same customary business management practices, principles and philosophies that created this mess. So I began a search for a new platform that owners and managers could utilize that would fully recognize the importance of balanced and fair "exchanges", and also incorporate new ideas related to redefining business success, business competition, business leadership and much, much more.

Mother Nature – A model for business success?

I'm one of those guys who has had a lot of luck. When I started my ad agency I was lucky to pick up my first big client within 60 days of putting out my shingle (that client stuck with us until I sold the agency over 22 years later!). And when the agency started having good luck in winning regional and national creative awards, our growth became exponential. So it didn't surprise me when early on in my search for a new paradigm that would improve the way we manage and run our businesses, I stumbled upon the following quote from Albert Einstein: "Look to nature and you will understand everything better."

Eureka! By providing business leaders with simple vignettes from the natural world and linking them to situations in the business world, maybe they will begin to not only see themselves and the businesses they run in new and different ways, but they might begin to think, plan and act differently as well. But if the primordial character of nature is "survival of the fittest" as Charles Darwin hypothesized, how could a book that utilizes metaphors and lessons from the natural world lead us out of this management, leadership and financial mess? Didn't intense competition and survival of the fittest get us to where we are today?

Mother Nature - Survival of the fittest?

While Darwin is the most famous evolutionist, the true pioneer and founder of the theory of evolution was the French biologist Jean-Baptiste de Lamarck. His theory, which was presented 50 years before Darwin, was based on an "instructive", cooperative interaction among organisms and their environment that enables living organisms to survive and evolve. It is a much more compassionate theory of survival that substitutes struggle and aggression with harmony and cooperation where the strong help the weak and in so doing all become stronger. A rapidly growing field called "Systems Biology" recognizes the critical role cooperation plays in sustaining life on earth. So I ask you to ponder the following question - Why wouldn't the "systems" principles that have created abundance in nature (biology) also apply to sustaining and growing business organizations? If that makes even a little bit of sense to you, I think you're going to enjoy this book.

Who should read this book?

I wrote this book primarily for owners, managers, supervisors and soon-to-be supervisors in small to medium-sized businesses. Non-fiction authors are supposed to write what they know about, and for many years my ad agency employed 65 people with annual sales revenue of over $10 million, which is classified by the Small Business Administration as a medium-sized business. Over the years I also had the opportunity to work for a number of small to medium-sized business, so I've witnessed the good, the bad and the ugly from the perspective of an employee as well as an owner/manager.

This book was also written for college graduates who are entering the workforce in positions well above the summer job positions they've previously held. Looking back on my own career, I wish a book like this was available to me after graduation because I was thrown into supervisory positions with absolutely no mentoring or practical management advice what-so-ever. Yes, my college professors provided me with a wealth of intellectual information about planning, leading and managing employees, but nobody provided me with rubber-hit-the-road tips about negotiating, personal selling techniques or how to conduct effective employee performance reviews. A quote by Mark Twain comes to mind when I consider those years, "The first half of my life I went to school. The second half of my life I got an education." So I hope this book serves as a quick education for those college graduates who feel like they need one.

How to get the most out of this book

There are a total of 88 business lessons. Knowing that business executives and supervisors are time starved, and utilizing my advertising agency training and background, each lesson will take you less than a minute to read. Like great advertising or poetry, for that matter, you will soon discover that the brevity of each lesson does not reflect the amount of knowledge compacted into each page. So I encourage you to go ahead and read through the entire book quickly, but after you've done so, read and put into practice one lesson a day. I also suggest that you access the wealth of information associated with each lesson provided in the resources section at the back of the book.

What you should know about me – Attitudes, opinions, beliefs

In the wake of the current corporate leadership and management scandals the notion of greater business transparency has been advocated by private citizens and government officials, alike. For me, the definition implies openness and access to important information. And what's more important to someone who is seeking advice than knowing the biases and worldview of the person who is shelling out the advice? So I thought I'd share the philosophies and notions that I have about business and about life upfront so you can compare them to your own and determine whether the ideas and recommendations provided in this book are of any value to you. Here's how I see things:

- People want to be part of something bigger than they can create on their own.
- Everything is connected; therefore there is no separation between an individual's "personal" life and their life in business.
- We are all connected to the ocean no matter where you live what's more; we are totally dependent upon its health for our own health.
- Most people are insecure and lead fear-based lives; therefore it is a supervisor's responsibility to work through their own fears and then help employees work through theirs.
- More can be accomplished in business through cooperation than through competition.
- Mother Nature has her limits and we are fast approaching them.
- There is no such thing as perfect communication.
- People take the easiest route … and for some people the easy route is the hardest.
- Most business people suffer from nature deficit disorder.
- Metaphors force people to go to a deeper level of consciousness and understanding.
- Rules and company policies don't kill employee morale and creativity, supervisors do.
- Intuition is undervalued in most business decisions.
- A typical executive spends nearly 1 ½ days (30%) of a 5-day work week sorting, reading, filing, writing, sending and recovering from email messages.
- In the absence of information people will make up their own story.
- Measure twice, cut once.
- Failure is good if you learn something from it.
- Nature does not know the concept of waste.
- The one and only thing you can control in life is your reaction to "the outside world".
- Most companies, particularly small to medium-sized companies, are the shadow of the person who is leading it.
- First be a good animal.

What's with the crazy book title - how did you come up with it?

Life is a journey and 10 years ago that journey became an inward exploration of my conscious and sub-conscious thoughts. Early on I discovered that despite appearances of success and business accomplishments, my self-esteem and confidence were actually quite low. In a word, I felt insecure and as I began to deal with my situation I wondered if everybody around me was truly as confident and self-assured as they appeared to be.

I concluded the only way to find out was to ask, so I started having deep discussions with many of my friends and relatives. Eventually, I talked with hundreds of top executives in major corporations, business associates and strangers and guess what … they all felt insecure in many aspects of their lives. All of which may not be a big surprise to psychologists or psychiatrists, but it sure was to me.

So when I came across the following quote by Jacob Braude – "People are like ducks … calm and unruffled on the surface but paddling like the devil underneath." – I not only decided to make it the platform from which all the recommendations and ideas presented in my book would be launched from, but I decided to adapt it as the title. Put simply, as a business owner, manager or supervisor the only thing you really need to know is that people are unsure of themselves and truly successful businessmen and women do whatever it takes to mitigate rather than exploit that trait in the people they work with.

Hey, maybe the title isn't so crazy after all!

CHAPTER 1

Business Philosophy

Nature

"**W**e need the tonic of wildness, to wade sometimes in marshes where the bittern and the meadow-hen lurk, and hear the booming of the snipe; to smell the whispering sedge where only some wilder and more solitary fowl builds her nest, and the mink crawls with its belly close to the ground." – Henry David Thoreau

---

Business Lesson

The healing power of nature; some scientists believe the restorative ability of nature might even be hardwired into man. In recent studies psychologists have found that exposure to trees, streams and other natural features quiets the mind, improves concentration, increases creativity and boosts self-esteem. Stephen and Rachel Kaplan, psychologists at the University of Michigan, found in their studies that workers who have nature views from their office or cubical are more enthusiastic about their jobs, less frustrated, in better health and more satisfied with their lives. And in a separate study Virginia Lohr, Washington State University, found that blood pressure, pulse rates and concentration of office workers was positively affected by indoor office plants. So if you're looking to improve your attitude, your personal performance or the attitudes and performance of your employees, simply tap into Mother Nature.

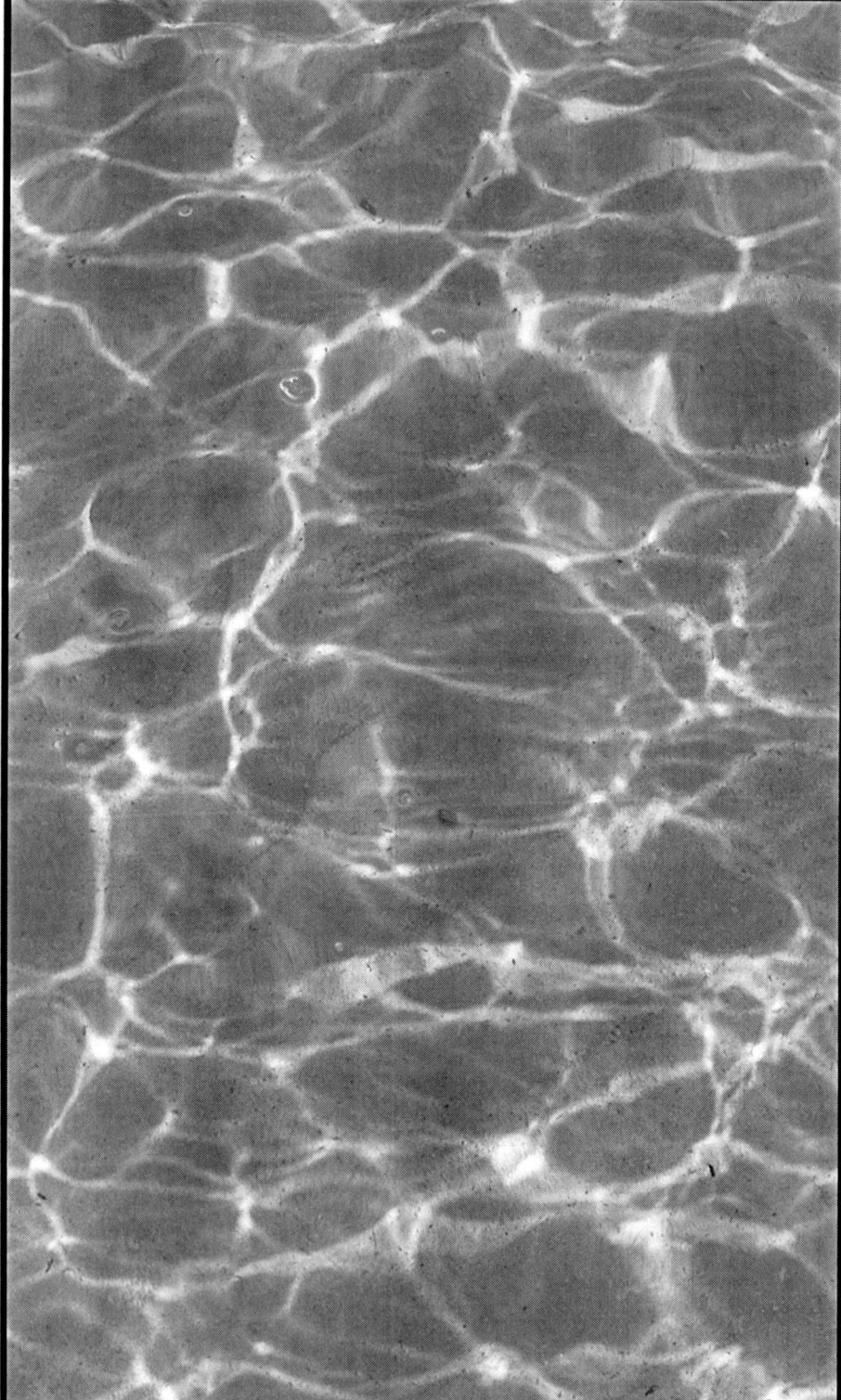

Nature

"The world's water is our life support system. We're all connected to the ocean no matter where we live, and completely depend on its health for our own health. All water, whether it is salt or fresh water, is connected because the ocean's water evaporates into the atmosphere, becomes snow on the mountains, melts and trickles down the mountains into rivers and streams and is then carried back into the ocean. And it arrives there with everything toxic that we put into it, because we continue to use the ocean as a garbage can." – Jean-Michel Cousteau

---

Business Lesson

When college students or people who are entering the business world ask me to provide them with the best piece of business advice I've ever received, my answer reflects Jean-Michel Cousteau's observation – what comes around goes around. If you're engaged in ruthless, shady or unethical business practices those toxic ways of conducting business are going to find their way back to you. On the other hand, if you are supportive in what you do and if your products and services provide genuine value, those attributes will trickle back to you in the people and the customers you attract. Somehow, someway, it's all connected.

Nature

Staring out the kitchen window my eyes were drawn to a small area next to our backyard fence where two chipmunks were tumbling and tussling. The action only lasted half a minute but what an explosion of energy! Afterward the loser dashed quickly away while the other calmly went back to searching for food. The victor seemed so serene I began to question whether I had imagined the squabble.

Business Lesson

After a fight with another wild animal I don't think critters go away saying to themselves, "That was a cheap shot – if I had only seen it coming I would have kicked his ass. The next time I see him I'm going to make him pay, big time!" Carrying a grudge or a vendetta takes a lot of energy … energy that could be spent more productively by taking care of your existing customers, soliciting new ones or simply complimenting a co-worker on a job well done. Choose how you expend your energy wisely.

Nature

The cheetah catches up to 60% of the prey it hunts, the lion has less than a 30% success rate, while the Little Eagle (native to Australia and New Guinea) has only a 15% hunting success rate.

Business Lesson

We can learn a couple of things from the cheetah, the lion and the Little Eagle. First, persistence is an important component of success. When I made "cold" telephone calls to Porter & Associates prospects during the first six months after I opened the agency, my success rate (successfully set an appointment to meet face to face with the prospect) was around 20% … on a good day! If I hadn't continued to call prospects and re-call those who turned me down, my agency would not have survived. Secondly, I imagine wild animals learn something from their failures … so do people. Think about this: if all you experience in business is success after success after success, how would you learn anything new? So failure is good, if you learn something from it. Unfortunately most people in business don't view it as an opportunity to grow emotionally and intellectually, and they assign attributes and judgments such a "loser", "underachiever" and "low performer" to those who experience failure. All of which is why many businesses produce mediocre results … fear of failure.

Nature

Some coast redwood trees are more than 375 feet tall. By contrast, redwood cones are only an inch long. Each cone contains 14-24 tiny seeds … it would take over 100,000 seeds to weigh a pound.
– *Save The Redwoods League*

Business Lesson

George Leonard, author of twelve books, former senior editor of *Look Magazine,* fifth-degree black belt in aikido and founder of Leonard Energy Training (LET) must have been inspired by a redwood seed when he said, "Whatever your age, your upbringing, or your education, what you are made of is mostly unused potential." If only more of our leaders and managers in business would view their employees in that way, what a change in productivity, in company culture and in job satisfaction American business would experience.

Nature

Studies of Bonobo Chimpanzes in the wild and in captivity reveal that there is no lethal aggression between Bonobos. Put succintly, Bonobos do not wage war.

Business Lesson

Many of the people that I have been associated with in business use war as an anology for the way they do business. Even the language they use supports a military approach: we're launching a marketing campaign, our new product is going to kill theirs, we've got to out flank them … and eveybody has heard about the cola wars, burger wars and beer wars! I'm not advocating that competitors should make love, not war (as the Bonobos do, by the way). But I am suggesting that we create a more productive competitive atmosphere by implementing a mindset that our best Olympic athletes demonstrate when the gold medal winner invites the silver and bronze medal competitors to stand up on the gold platform. This gesture is recognition that the competition among the athletes improved the gold medal winners performance, and indeed the level of performance for everyone.

Nature

In all the time I have spent on oceans, lakes and streams; and in forests, deserts and mountains throughout the world; in the corn and soybean fields of Iowa and the hundreds or thousands of hours that I have spent watching the Nature Channel, I have yet to witness a wild animal multi-tasking.

Business Lesson

Wild animals seem to have a singular focus in everything they do. I doubt if a mother lion would be successful in either endeavor if she combined nursing her cubs with hunting down prey. I agree with the person who said, "Multitasking is the art of distracting yourself from two things you'd rather not be doing by doing them simultaneously." New scientific studies reveal the inefficiencies and hidden costs of people's attempts to do more than one thing at a time. Besides, it only increases the craziness in your business and social life … so find the courage to act like a lion – don't multi-task.

Nature

Elephants don't bite!

Business Lesson

Many years ago shortly after I opened my advertising agency I mailed a postcard to my list of prospects. The headline was … Elephants Don't Bite. The copy was a reminder that throughout the history of humankind, man has never, ever been bitten by an elephant. However, literally millions upon millions of people have been bitten by mosquitoes. The moral of the story was it's the little things that will "get you" in business. Pay attention to all the details involved in a project (or your position responsibilities) and the big things will take care of themselves. Looking back, that was pretty good advice.

Nature

Interdependence between all things in nature is obvious even to people who have not spent much time outdoors. Whether you consider the interdependency between a coral reef and the quality of the ocean water that surrounds it, or the relationship between levels of carbon dioxide in our atmosphere and global warming … everything is connected.

Business Lesson

Many business people do not give consideration to the concept of "connectedness" and the potential effects of their actions. I've heard well-meaning busy executives say that everything is moving so fast, they don't have time to sit and ponder all the ramifications of their decisions. I've heard others admit that they don't really care who or what might be affected – get tough or get out. For those who are willing to examine the dynamics of interdependence, here's an idea: Before announcing a change, particularly a major one, ask yourself three questions: (1) Would my mother be proud of me in what I'm about to do or say? (2) Who will be affected and what is my responsibility to them? (3) What's the worst thing that can happen, long-range and short-term, as a result of my action(s)?

Nature

After you've been motoring away from your camp for about 30 minutes, all the islands on Canadian lakes begin to look the same. Unless you're really paying attention, and unless you are naturally grounded in a good sense of direction it's easy to get lost. Even experienced guides carry an extra book of matches with them at all times … just in case they can't find their way home and have to spend the night on the lake.

Business Lesson

It's easy to lose your way in the business world. Unless an individual has taken time to examine and reflect upon their personal values, it might be easy to overlook business decisions that have the potential to destroy careers, reputations and other things people have worked hard to create. Individuals who live their lives from a deep under-standing of who they are experience less stress, more success and indeed more joy in their work by simply knowing they are on course and in integrity.

CHAPTER 2

Managing/Supervising/Leadership

Nature

Water flowing downhill follows the path of least resistance.

Business Lesson

Robert Fritz, in his book *The Path of Least Resistance for Managers* (1999) proposes that the energy of an organization travels down the path of least resistance. And if an organization is not realizing the results it is seeking, management can redesign the organizational structure and redirect the flow in the direction they want it to go. In his "nine laws of organizational structure" Fritz suggests that while change initiatives within a company may appear to be successful, if an organization's structure remains unchanged its behavior will revert to its previous behavior. So if your company isn't achieving the results you're after, maybe it's the underlying structure that's keeping you from advancing. Maybe it's time to create a new path of least resistance.

Nature

Vultures don't delegate ... they do their own dirty work.

Business Lesson

Sometimes people do things through others that they wouldn't have done if they were in direct contact with the people or person who is affected. All kinds of psychological studies have been conducted that reveal this. Remember the experiments where a subject was more likely to shock a victim if he or she was allowed to administer the shock through another person (secondary agent)? Cause and effect is the basis of reality, and when we distance ourselves from our effects by delegating "dirty work" to a lawyer or a vice president or a manager, apparently we somehow create an illusion that we are off the hook with regard to the consequences. Which is why I believe people who are in powerful positions should do their own dirty work by looking a person in the eyes and telling him he is fired. Or by gathering all affected employees and personally announcing that you are closing their branch. Delegation to others is important in growing a successful business. But when it comes to decisions that could be harmful or detrimental to others, trying to keep you hands clean is the wrong route to go.

Nature

Some cocoons have built-in lines of weakness that help a butterfly emerge from its chrysalis. If, however, the emerging insect is able to escape too easily, its wings may never fully develop.

Business Lesson

If you watch a butterfly attempting to escape from its cocoon it will look like a difficult struggle. But an entomologist will tell you that the movement and energy required to split the cocoon are important toward the development of a healthy insect. I carefully watched people who reported to me struggle with new assignments, new responsibilities and with new challenges and I learned early on not to intervene too quickly. Allowing others to struggle with decisions or other aspects of their job strengthens their character and resolve. I have witnessed many well-meaning managers jump too soon into a situation and they robbed the individual of a valuable learning opportunity.

Nature

On the topic of feedback loops, Dr. Richard Zeebe, faculty member in the Department of Oceanography at the University of Hawaii commented on the climate's ability to remove carbon dioxide from the atmosphere: *"These feedbacks operate so slowly that they will not help us in terms of climate change [...] that we're going to see in the next several hundred years. Right now we have put the system entirely out of equilibrium."*

Business Lesson

Feedback loops in nature and in business serve an important purpose - should something increase or decrease, other mechanisms are naturally triggered to bring the system back into equilibrium. Big problems occur, however, when these systems are overtaxed, so early warning systems and processes should be put into place in your business to insure timely detection. For example at Porter & Associates if billable hours fell 20% below our projections for a particular month, new business acquisition activities would automatically kick in. What area(s) of your business would benefit from establishment of a feedback loop(s)?

Nature

"People are like ducks ... calm and unruffled on the surface but paddling like the devil underneath." – Jacob Braude

---

Business Lesson

Deep down, most people are insecure. Whether it's insecurity in their relationships, in the economy, or in the work they do ... insecurity can permeate many areas of an individual's life. And rather than exploiting those insecurities to turn an extra profit or to achieve corporate goals, the best managers I've been associated with do what's necessary to mitigate employees' fears or uncertainties.

Nature

Humpback whales have developed a unique technique of feeding referred to as bubble net feeding: Once a group of humpbacks has located a large school of herring they swim in a circle beneath the school blowing bubbles and making vocalizations that panic the herring and condense the school. A cylinder-shaped curtain of ascending bubbles forms that creates a wall around the herring through which the school of fish will not pass. Next, humpbacks explode like missiles from the deep with mouths wide open gorging on herring. It is truly a spectacular act of teamwork and collaboration.

Business Lesson

To be effective, successful and profitable organizations need teamwork. Important lessons we can learn from bubble net feeding are: (1) It is important to think as one team (2) Teams are most effective if the group works on one single concept and (3) Clear communication among participants is crucial to success.

Nature

Geese are flying overhead. I have marveled at their V formation ever since I can remember. What I didn't realize until just recently is that geese switch in and out of the lead position not only because the point is the most strenuous (the leader needs to be spelled similar to how bikers draft one another in the Tour de France), but because no individual goose knows the entire migration route!

Business Lesson

Passing off leadership responsibility among a group goes against the advice of most of the books on leadership that I have read. But most of those books were written years ago, when members of a department or project team were all neatly located within the confines of a particular building or city. And it was before business problems became as complex as they sometimes are today. So think about passing the leadership baton among group members the next time you are assigned to a project team. You'll be taking group collaboration to a whole new level and who knows … maybe your solutions will be more imaginative and at a higher level, as well.

Nature

Busy as a bee. I'm witnessing it in this moment. It's early morning, the sun is just now rising and bees are visiting the Black-Eyed Susan's. Jumping from flower to flower with wings beating at pretty close to a zillion miles per hour – they're surely going to wear themselves out before long. I wonder how they do it … where do they get all that energy?

Business Lesson

I worked for a guy who got to work before 7:00 am every morning. He left work relatively early (around 4:00 pm) mainly, I think, to beat the traffic so he could get home quickly and start working again. I received e-mails at all hours of the evening, during holidays, while he was on vacation … and that was before he bought a Blackberry! All of us used to marvel at his endurance, but mostly we questioned his sanity. Like the bees, he was probably just doing what he was born to do. He also had a very clear sense of "mission" in his life, and a good sense of purpose – so putting in all those hours was probably more joy than work. Some people are just "built" to work like the dickens. For them, working less simply isn't an option. And if they're smart, they'll recognize their uniqueness and won't expect the same of others.

Nature

The weather this summer has been remarkable so the forest is green and lush with wild flowers, underbrush and leaves galore. In a word the forest today is displaying abundance. And what strikes me is the idea that even if we were in a drought and everything was brittle and brown from the lack of moisture … abundance would remain but in the form of potential.

Business Lesson

In the late part of my business career helping those who reported to me reach their potential became a responsibility rather than an option. And the moment I accepted that responsibility everything changed. Attitudes improved, performance improved and corporate life was just more pleasant. If I had it all to do over again I'd draw up contracts with each of the people who report to me that would spell out our responsibilities to each other. My portion of each and every contract would read: I pledge to do my best to help you achieve your potential in your position and as a human being.

Nature

I took a walk in the woods this morning with an individual that I am mentoring. When I asked him to share what he was seeing and what he was hearing I was reminded how differently each and every one of us sees and experiences the world. The trees that he pointed out were not the trees that had caught my attention. And the insect and animal sounds he had heard didn't come to my attention until he mentioned them. But what was most interesting was his apology for not seeing and hearing things as I did.

Business Lesson

I have found that the people who are most successful in business are open to the ideas of others and genuinely try to see things from their point of view. There's a tendency in life and particularly in business for people to make others wrong so they can be right. In doing so, alternative ways of solving a problem are sometimes quickly discarded, even before they have been fully examined. The best decisions are made when there is a full pool of options to choose from. People who have right-wrong issues drain the pool, and in doing so they devalue others opinions and contributions to the point where team members will either stop contributing their ideas … or they will apologize for bringing an idea to the table that is "different".

Nature

At age 5 or 6 my youngest son, Logan, and I were holding hands standing on the beach in front of our summer cottage. It was a windy day with huge waves on the lake. We had been standing there in silence for some time when he looked up to me and said, "The waves are the teeth of the lake." Out of the mouths of babes.

Business Lesson

To be effective all corporate policies and procedures must have clear consequences if an employee chooses not to abide by them. In short, they have to have "teeth" because many adults live their lives from the emotional intelligence of a child. Without consequences managers and supervisors will be deprived of a valuable management tool required to produce the results the company is after.

Nature

"**O**rangutans and bonobos are given the choice of whether they want to paint as an enrichment activity. Enrichment is not viewed as a separate activity for Great Ape Trust's orangutans and bonobos, but rather a philosophy of daily management and research. "– *Peter Clay, Senior Orangutan Caretaker, Great Ape Trust of Iowa*

Business Lesson

If the managers and supervisors within U.S. businesses were as committed to providing their employees with challenging, engaging and fulfilling activities as the caretakers at the Great Ape Trust are to offering them to captive apes - job satisfaction, company loyalty and creative acuity would soar. Job enrichment as it is typically thought of was developed in the 1950s by Frederick Herzberg, an American psychologist. Its purpose is to motivate employees by giving them the opportunity to use a broader range of their abilities by providing job variety, more autonomy and when necessary re-engineering job processes. In today's business world I feel the definition should be expanded to include training and education in areas including creative thinking and problem solving, emotional intelligence, teamwork and collaboration and how to get beyond limiting beliefs. Enrichment should be part of daily corporate life, just like it is at the Great Ape Trust of Iowa.

Nature

The mud wasps are really active today. Their flight patterns are as unpredictable as their temperament seems to be. While my rational mind tells me wasps are merely going about doing their thing, they sure appear to be menacing ... they scare the heck out of me!

Business Lesson

An important trait of a good leader is predictability. People feel safe working with a supervisor who is consistent in their words and actions. Fear is the result of un-predictability and while many business leaders "rule" their businesses and departments by striking fear into the hearts of those who report to them ... the managers who embrace compassionate leadership qualities produce superior results over the long haul.

Nature

Have you ever watched a mother goose mentor her goslings? When teaching them how to swim she will jump into the water ahead of them, and then carefully watch to be sure everyone has made it safely into the pond. If there is danger she will hide the entire brood in tall weeds or grass. And when it's feeding time she won't provide the meal but she will demonstrate how to dive to the bottom for the best morsels. When it comes to mentoring, geese do a great job.

Business Lesson

Mentoring is about providing help and support in a non-threatening way that will boost a mentee's confidence and empower them to move forward in a new way to achieve success. It's not surprising that in the fast-paced business world where everyone is frantically trying to meet or exceed profit goals, and/or doing more with less, mentoring of employees has taken a backseat. It's sad because watching and learning from somebody who has "been there done that" can be so productive and beneficial. I've heard that 80% of communication happens not in the words that are used but in the way things are said. I've also heard that demonstration is the most effective form of training. And when I've brought up the idea of initiating or reinvigorating a mentoring program to some of my clients I've heard it said, "We can't afford it!" And my response is, "You can't afford not to!"

MANAGING/SUPERVISING/LEADERSHIP

CHAPTER 3

Coporate Culture

Nature

Honey bee swarms are nature's way of packing up and moving. Overcrowding and congestion in the hive are the main reasons for bee colonies to swarm. When the bees leave their hive, the queen is in the center of the swarm protected by the other bees from predators and the weather. In short, swarming is a process that allows the colony to reproduce itself.

Business Lesson

Porter & Associates tried to reproduce itself by opening branch offices in two cities outside of our home state of Iowa. Neither location was successful. Looking back I think the primary reasons were because we did not successfully transfer and protect our corporate values, the company mission and the company culture. If you are a small to medium-sized business that's considering expansion by opening branches, be sure to protect the queen bee … the values, mission and culture of your organization.

Nature

Dolphins have been observed supporting sick or dying pod members.

Business Lesson

If managers and supervisors would simply set time aside during each work week to extend encouragement and support to their reports, they'd increase employee morale and cut down on employee turnover dramatically. Review just about any list of the most common reasons why employees quit their jobs, and being ignored and unappreciated will be at the top. How you demonstrate support of your colleagues and/or reports can range from writing a simple handwritten note of appreciation to stopping by their office and telling them one-on-one how much you value their contribution.

Nature

Trees help control erosion, provide shelter for birds and animals and control levels of carbon dioxide in the atmosphere. While all three of these attributes have big effects in the world, probably the most important is the last one because of its direct relationship with the earth's climate. One acre of trees removes 2.6 tons of CO_2 per year, thus helping to reduce the "greenhouse effect". If levels of carbon dioxide go out of balance, the earth's climate will fluctuate dramatically which would have a devastating impact on all species.

Business Lesson

Who represents the trees within your company? Who has the most influence over the business climate within your organization? Who has the most influence over employees' attitudes, opinions and beliefs related to the company mission, the company value proposition and to accountability within your organization? Who are the key people within your organization that possess the responsibility of controlling its culture? If your answer is anything other than the people sitting in the C-suites, it could be devastating.

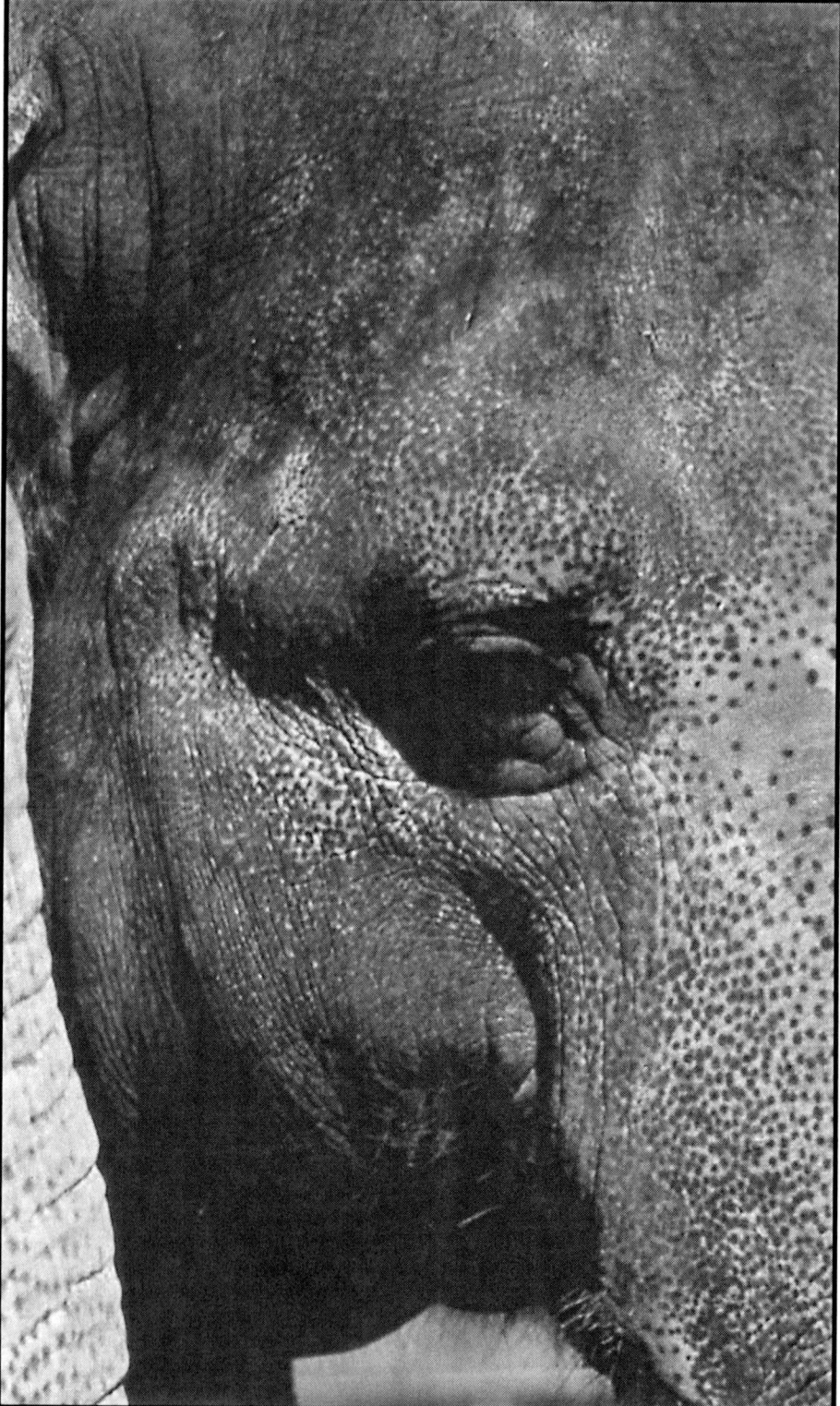

Nature

According to recent scientific research in evolutionary biology, cognitive ethnology and social neuroscience conducted by leading animal communication and cognition experts, there is now hard evidence that elephants have empathy.

Business Lesson

Bruna Martinuzzi, president and founder of Clarion Enterprises, a company that specializes in emotional intelligence and leadership training said, "There are numerous studies that link empathy to business results. They include studies that correlate empathy with increased sales, with the performance of the best managers of product development teams and with enhanced performance in an increasingly diverse workforce." With so many documented business benefits and hard, tangible results attributed to utilization of empathy in conducting business, why aren't more companies doing what the elephants do? What gains in employee morale, employee retention, customer satisfaction, customer loyalty and profitability do you think an organization would experience that fully integrated "empathy" into its daily practices and corporate values?

CHAPTER 4

Sustainability/Ecology

Nature

"Nature does not know the concept of waste; the only species capable of making something no one desires is the human species". – Zero Emissions Research and Initiatives (ZERI)

Business Lesson

"Waste results from the inefficient use of any resource and includes activities and products that generate by-products with no clear use, no market value, or hazardous properties". – Zero Waste Alliance. The amount of waste generated by U.S. businesses is earth shattering … literally. For starters, between 14 million to 20 million PCs are dumped each year in the United States, and worldwide, discarded computers now account for 5% of all waste. Although the total amount of waste generated, recycled, or disposed is not truly known (the EPA has not collected or confirmed that data, which by the way is a violation of federal requirements) it is widely accepted that we cannot continue interacting with the environment in the way we have in the past. To find out what you and your business can do to reduce or eliminate waste, go to the resources section at the back of this book.

Nature

Everything in the natural world is biodegradable … everything.

Business Lesson

According to the FTC, only products that contain materials that "break down and decompose into elements found in nature within a reasonably short amount of time when they are exposed to air, moisture and bacteria or other organisms" should be marketed as "biodegradable". So while more and more manufacturers are producing biodegradable products and materials, realistically only a very small percentage of our current consumer and industrial products will be converted into biodegradable or compostable form. So the next best thing we can do for our environment is to become more aware of the importance of recycling. Fortunately many consulting companies that specialize in reducing waste disposal and recycling costs are springing up through out the country. You can find a partial list of companies at the back of this book. And to motivate you to start or renew a recycling program in your company, I have provided (below) a list of common products and how long it takes them to degrade:

- Banana peel, 2 – 10 days
- Orange peels, 1 month
- Cotton rags, 1 – 5 months
- Paper, 2 – 5 months
- Cigarette filters, 1 – 12 years
- Plastic bags, 10 – 20 years

- Diapers, 200 – 500 years
- Leather shoes, 25 – 40 years
- Aluminum cans, 200 - 500 years
- Plastic bottles, 70 - 450 years
- XPS Foam cup, non-biodegradeable

Nature

Mother Nature has her limits … and we are fast approaching them.

Business Lesson

In their book *The Natural Step For Business* (1999) Brian Nattrass and Mary Altomare say, "Our industrial economy, indeed any human economy, is contained within and dependent upon the natural world. The natural world is not separate from the human economy. All of our basic life needs – breathing, drinking, and eating – are entirely dependent on the continuing capacity of the natural world to provide us with pure, uncontaminated air, water and food." They accurately point out that we are increasingly impairing nature's ability to provide us with these services, and propose a new framework and mental model of sustainable business development called The Natural Step that they have successfully integrated into four large corporations. Paul Hawken in his book *The Ecology of Commerce* (1994) provides a picture of business as it could be if only we, as leaders in the business world, would make the right choices: "We have the capacity and ability to create a remarkably different economy, one that can restore ecosystems and protect the environment while bringing forth innovation, prosperity, meaningful work, and true security. The restorative economy unites ecology and commerce into one sustainable act of production and distribution that mimics and enhances natural processes."

CHAPTER 5

Control/Change

Nature

Balance of nature is a term for an ideal condition in which the interrelationships and inherent equilibrium of organisms, plants and animals interacting to one another and their environment appear harmonious. In reality, the balance is continually upset by natural events.

Business Lesson

When things get out of balance and don't go as planned, many business people, particularly those who have "control issues" tend to fly off the handle (I speak from experience, just ask anyone who worked for me particularly early-on in my career). A less stressful, more reality-based way to "do" business is to recognize that in business, as in nature, out of balance (out of control) is occurring continually. Most likely, your ego won't allow you to recognize it. But the part of you connected to Mother Nature knows that events are sure to happen within your department, your company and/or your industry that may threaten and possibly destroy the balance you worked so hard to establish. My advice? Be flexible and find a way to enjoy it.

CONTROL/CHANGE

Nature

I was 14-years old and the last thing I yelled to my older brother before our sailboat, an M-16, capsized was, "I've got everything under control!" At that moment a 20 mile-an-hour gust filled our sails and a 10 ft high wave crashed into our port side instantly flipping us into the lake. Dazed and a little embarrassed, I sensed that I'd just received a lesson from Mother Nature. When you're on a lake in a sailboat, ultimately the wind and the waves are in control and you're just along for the ride.

Business Lesson

Put your key in the ignition, turn it and your car starts. Compose a message, hit the send button and your e-mail is instantly delivered. We experience so many things in our lives where we are so clearly in control that we begin to believe we possess the power to control the outcome for nearly everything. But beware. That surge in company sales may not be related to the ad campaign you authorized, and while you may feel you deserve your promotion, you may have received it for reasons you may never be made aware of. So if you want to make your ride a little bit smoother integrate the following truth: the one and only thing you can control in business (and in life) is your reaction to the things that are going on around you.

CONTROL/CHANGE

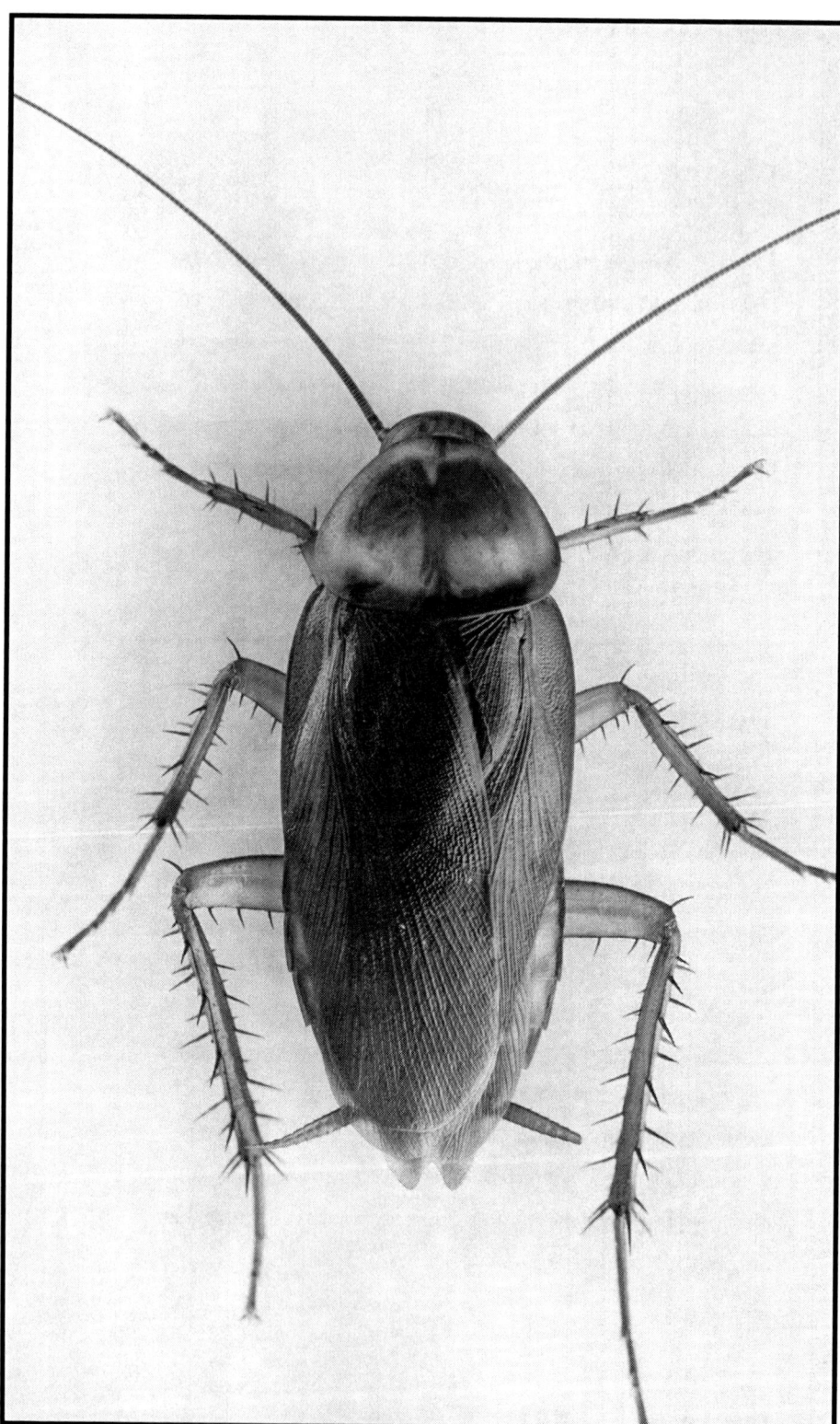

Nature

Cockroach-like fossils have been discovered from the Carboniferous period which was between 295-354 million years ago. Talk about a critter that's capable of adjusting and thriving in changing conditions!

Business Lesson

My ad agency did promotional work for a company that was once known as the most innovative manufacturer in its industry. But, as time went by, and as the people in top management changed, the company's commitment to change and innovation waned until it found itself in a situation where nearly all of their patents had expired … which is when they called my agency in to save the day. I believed then as I believe now that when it comes to success there is no substitute for a truly great product; a product that completely meets the needs of the market or better yet, meets the needs of a segment of the market. If management had committed to continuously adapt to the changing needs of its customers, if they would have taken a lesson from cockroaches, the company would have continued to be unrivaled in the industry. Product Leadership (innovation year after year) is one of three market leadership disciplines identified by Michael Treacy and Fred Wiersema in their book *The Discipline of Market Leaders* (1997). Should change and innovation be your company's value discipline?

CONTROL/CHANGE

Nature

Weather …in Iowa you can count on it to change. Over the course of three hours yesterday afternoon, the temperature dropped 16 degrees. At 1:00 pm when it was 88 degrees I was wearing shorts and a T-shirt but by 4:00 pm it was 72 degrees so I was in jeans and a sweatshirt. I ran some late afternoon errands and couldn't help but notice how a majority of the shoppers were still wearing flip-flops and tank-tops. Didn't they notice the change in the weather?

Business Lesson

Things change in business, sometimes as rapidly as the weather in Iowa. Within 12 months the No.1 and No.2 companies in an industry I'm familiar with were sold and completely changed their business strategies and direction. And the top executives of the company in fourth position made some poor business policy decisions and were on the verge of bankruptcy. What did the No.3 company do in response? Nothing … it maintained its marketing plan, sales goals, corporate goals, strategic objectives – you name it, everything remained exactly as it had been laid out at the annual planning meeting. Sometimes doing nothing in response to competitor's changes makes a lot of sense – sometimes it doesn't. My advice is to error on the side of making change.

CONTROL/CHANGE

CHAPTER 6

Work-Life Balance

Nature

Rocky Mountain Big Horn Sheep are known for their perfect sense of balance. They use ledges only 2 inches wide for footholds and can run up mountain slopes at 15 mph. Jumping from ledge to ledge over crevasses as wide as 20 feet is common.

Business Lesson

Finding work-life balance in today's fast-paced, what-have-you-done-for-me-today world can be precarious. What might be good for your advancement within your company could lead to uncertain consequences within your marriage, and what might be beneficial to strengthening your family relationships could be perilous to your business career. What's worse is if things are out of balance for an extended period of time, it can be dangerous to your health, your co-workers and to your family. Five tips provided by WebMD for achieving better work-life balance are: (1) Figure out what really matters to you in life, (2) Drop unnecessary activities, (3) Protect your private time, (4) Accept help to balance your life, and (5) Plan fun and relaxation. For more information about work-life balance, go to the resources section of this book.

Nature

A few months ago while fishing for Marlin we came upon a large pod of Spinner Dolphins hard at work chasing and relentlessly feeding on mackerel. So you can imagine my surprise when 20-30 Spinners broke from the group and swam over to have some fun riding on the bow wave of our boat. Their visit was relatively brief, 5-10 minutes, but like a carnival ride I imagine it was a fun and even an invigorating break!

Business Lesson

Working hard in our business society is revered and admired. I have overheard old-timers advise new employees to not worry about their salary or job title and to simply work hard and eventually they'll achieve their dreams. I agree with those words of advice, but I would also add the following ... "and don't forget to take time out to play." Some people are lucky enough to be in positions where their work is like play – but for most employees work is ...work. Nobody has ever come up with a truly creative idea while they were stressed-out, so whether it's taking 10-15 minute breaks during the day or a 2-week vacation, be like a dolphin - stop working and have some fun!

Nature

Sailing aboard a small cruise ship somewhere in the Caribbean Sea between Barbados and St. Martin, my wife and I left our dinner table for a stroll on the back deck. As we gazed up at the stars an identical thought jumped into both of our heads … we're insignificant; merely a speck! I suspect our epiphany would not have been nearly as powerful had we experienced it on land. The power of the ocean … very grounding, very humbling.

Business Lesson

When it comes to "conducting business", it's important to keep a holistic perspective. When there are monthly financial and sales goals that need to be attained, and clients who have expectations well beyond anything ever promised to them, there is a tendency to become frustrated, stressed-out and short tempered. Amid it all it's hard to remember that in the end … I'm talking the very end of your life on this planet … what you accomplished in your "business life" will most likely be insignificant.

CHAPTER 7

Human Resources

Nature

According to Chinese philosophy there are five basic forms of energy: Fire, Earth, Metal, Water, and Wood. The five elements are symbolic for the different phases, or primal forces within the universe, nature and our bodies. Each element is also attributed to a certain personality archetype. Knowing which element(s) influence our personalities can help an individual negotiate life's journey in a more effective and meaningful manner.

Business Lesson

Sophisticated HR departments have been utilizing various testing methods to aid in vetting job applicants for many years. Two of the most common assessments are the Myers-Briggs Type Indicator and the DISC assessment (DISC is an acronym for: Dominance, Influence, Steadiness and Conscientiousness). Based upon the assumption that better decisions are made with more (as opposed to less) data, I recommend in addition to whatever an HR department is currently utilizing, additional insights might be gained by utilizing assessments based upon the five element theory. After all, Myers-Briggs and DISC are based upon information made available in the 1930's while the Chinese assessments are based upon elements that have been around forever!

Nature

Horses are prey animals. As such they have evolved into expert readers of energy. Horses mirror exactly what human body language is telling them.

Business Lesson

If you're acting nervous around a horse, the horse will become nervous. And if you're angry but have a smile on your face, the horse will read your "honest" emotion and shy away. Wisdom Horse Coaching, based in Minneapolis, partners with horses to help their clients discover productive and unproductive personality and behavioral patterns that are helping or inhibiting them from reaching their goals. Here's an excerpt from an article about how it works: Jim was hoping to land bigger clients, but found, through brushing Big Rusty, that he froze, brushing the same place over and over on Rusty's neck. Rusty became so annoyed that Lynn Baskfield, certified life and business coach, asked Jim to stop for a while, breathe and feel his body, then go back to brushing. His stokes became long and smooth. Within minutes, Rusty's head dropped in contentment. Rusty helped Jim see that he froze with his bigger clients, how he could step back when necessary, recognize what was needed and go back with confidence to create success. Equine Guided Coaching … give it a try!

Nature

In his book, *Introduction to Forestry Economics* (1990), Peter H. Pearse, Professor of Forest Resource Management at the University of British Columbia wrote about the Law of Diminishing Marginal Substitutability: "As more of one input is substituted for another; it takes larger and larger increments of it to maintain the same level of output."

Business Lesson

What if the laws of forestry economics also apply to American business economics? Consider this: American businesses are not fully recognizing the potential impact retiring baby boomers will have on their bottom lines. When senior executives and managers/directors exit the company via retirement, the skills and knowledge they possess go out the door with them. Very few companies have even assessed the possibility of the talent shortage caused by retirements, and even fewer have projected costs associated with recruiting new, younger workers. Knowledge is a critical strategic element that determines competitive advantage. How is your company going to mitigate the skill and knowledge gaps caused by baby boomer retirements? Can younger talent completely fill the gap created by experienced, older workers?

HUMAN RESOURCES

Nature

There isn't a ripple in the water above the creek bend today; it seems perfectly still. But when the water flows through the narrows of the bend below, it's transformed into turbulent, raging waves of energy. It's remarkable how such a slight change can initiate so much momentum.

Business Lesson

Michael Watkins, Associate Professor of Business Administration at Harvard Business School discussed the importance of creating momentum within a department or an organization in his book *The First 90 Days* (2003). "Failure to create momentum during your first few months virtually guarantees an uphill battle for the rest of your tenure in the job," according to Watkins. Based on three years of research into leadership transitions he provides a process and important tools that can be applied by a new CEO or a first-time manager. Be the bend in the creek!

Nature

I was about to squash a dragonfly on the first morning out of a month-long canoe trip when my camp counselor rushed over and informed me that dragonflies are a camper's best friend. "Why?", I asked. "Because they eat 10 times their weight in mosquitoes everyday." At age 14 the concept of friend or foe took on new meaning for me.

Business Lesson

When you're starting a new job its tough to determine who's going to be a friend and who might turn out to be your foe. Here's a way to cut through a person's façade and get a feel for their character. Take them out for dinner, but be sure to have them bring their spouse or significant other along. Then watch and listen and pay close attention to how he or she is treating the other. I did this with a prospective creative director, and I knew after 10 minutes he wasn't going to be anybody's friend at my company because I wasn't going to hire him … he wasn't even friendly with his wife.

CHAPTER 8

Communication

Nature

Honeybees use waggle dances to communicate both direction and distance of food sources.

Business Lesson

The business lesson we can learn from the waggle dance is 1-way communication can be very effective and efficient. Most people have been lead to believe that 2-way communication is always necessary. But when it comes to communication in business today one of the biggest nuisances is the ever increasing high volume of email messages. The fact is, a majority of email messages (especially interoffice messages) are actually 1-way messages that don't require a response, but because the sender doesn't tell recipients that a response isn't necessary, people waste literally thousands of hours composing them. So if you want to improve the effectiveness of email within your organization, and relieve a lot of stress, include the following words in the subject line of your email message if it applies: No Response Necessary! To learn more about email etiquette go to the resources section in the back of this book.

Nature

Body language in coral snakes is undeniable. With bright colors and flashy patterns poisonous animals like the coral snake are sending the message, "Look at me, I don't need to hide because I know you can't hurt me."

Business Lesson

Most psychologists agree that over 80% of communication happens not in the words that are used, but in the way things are said. According to Albert Mehrabian, in *Psychology Today* (1968) referring to a personal spoken message - 7% is conveyed by words; 38% by the vocal tones, and 55% by facial and body expressions. (By the way, if there is a conflict between the words someone is using and their body language, believe the body language!). Reading body language is an essential skill in "doing business" today and sadly, many of the companies I have worked with aren't providing the training and education necessary so their employees and sales people can utilize it, effectively. If you're interested in improving your ability to read body language go to the resources section at the back of this book.

Nature

Jaguars are territorial. Like other big cats the jaguar is solitary and males generally carve out large territories (50-80 square kilometers). Scrape marks, urine and scat are used to mark territories.

Business Lesson

Just like wild animals, we claim our territory in unique ways. The difference is humans sometimes mark territory unconsciously. Here are some territorial claim behaviors to be on the look-out for in yourself and others (provided by Max Widemen, internationally recognized speaker, engineer and expert on project management): Feet on desk, feet on chair, leaning against or touching an object, placing an object in a desired space, elevating oneself, and leaning back with hands behind head. Another aspect of territorial-ism was developed by American anthropologist Edward T. Hall which is referred to as "Proxemics". He determined that there are four different boundaries humans establish as protective zones surrounding ourselves: (1) Intimate Zone -18 inches around our body used for whispering and embracing, (2) Personal Zone – 18 inches to 4 feet used for conversing with close friends, (3) Social Zone – 4 to 10 feet used for conversing with acquaintances, and (4) Public Zone – 10 to 25 feet used for interacting with strangers. The business lesson? Honor the territories of others – invading another person's territory could carry dire consequences.

Nature

The Cicadas are singing all-out this evening. I've been told some can produce sound at 120 decibels (a chain saw is only 100 decibels). I wonder what message the sender is communicating and how the listener creates "meaning" from the songs. What are they listening to - is it the rhythm, the magnitude of the sound, the pitch … or is it something else entirely?

Business Lesson

How Cicadas create "meaning" from the sounds made by other Cicadas remains a mystery. Similarly, how humans create meaning from the "outside world" was a puzzle until the early 1970s when Neuro-Linguistic Programming (NLP) came onto the scene. The basic principle of NLP is that three elements create our perception of the world: a person's thoughts, gestures and words. Knowing your preferences as to how you filter incoming information is an important discovery toward being a better listener and communicator. For example, some people are auditory digital (focus on discrete words, facts, figures and logic) while others are auditory tonal (focus on subtle changes in a person's tone of voice). Knowing that you are auditory digital and a subordinate is auditory tonal, how would you change the way you communicate with them? If you're interested in learning more about NLP, go to the back of this book.

COMMUNICATION

Nature

Each species of birds speaks its own language. American Robins call back and forth among themselves as do Eastern Bluebirds and North American Orioles. But other than calls of distress or warning, I don't think birds outside a particular species understand what is being communicated.

Business Lesson

Industries and companies create their own language or "shop talk". During my first month of employment with an insurance company I remember secretly writing down the words and acronyms I didn't understand after meeting with my fellow officers and employees. At the end of the month I had a list of terms and phrases that completely filled both sides of an 8 ½" x 11" sheet of paper! So be aware, particularly with new employees and especially when your communications reach audiences outside your industry – most likely, you are not speaking "their" language. Convert your shop talk to something everyone can understand by asking individuals from outside your company (and your industry) to read and/or listen to what you have to say. And if anybody asks where you got this tip tell them a little bird told you.

Nature

I'm listening to a squirrel chattering away right now. Actually I've been listening to it for the past 25 minutes. It's inconceivable how it can keep that incessant noise going and going and going.

Business Lesson

There seems to be at least one person in every business who has the gift of gab … only when it comes to trying to get your work done, their gift is definitely not good for you. Lot's of people have "like me disease" so they get locked into conversations they'd really rather not be in. So when the office gossiper jumps into your cubical, do this: stand up immediately and remain standing throughout the entire conversation … you'll be amazed at the brevity of their stay.

Nature

There's lots of scat on the trail today. I've heard all kinds of stories about fox living in the center of the city, but because I've never seen or encountered first-hand evidence of them, I've always considered them to be just stories ... until today.

Business Lesson

There's a little storytelling in everything we say. Remember playing the game of telephone? You whisper something to the person next to you, and then they whisper it to the person next to them and so on until the message finally reaches the last person. In all the times I've played, the story at the very end is never, ever the original story - usually it's not even close. The Neuro-Linguistic Programming (NLP) model of communications outlines how information and events are filtered through our senses and as a result we delete, distort and generalize incoming data. So when you think you know the details of an incident, or a situation that has occurred within your company (or department) assume you're listening to a story ... and talk directly to the source.

CHAPTER 9

Personal Selling

Nature

To gain favorable attention and to win over females, male peacocks fan out their beautiful train of iridescent feathers in a magnificent display of courtship unmatched by any other species.

Business Lesson

The best sales people I've known possess just the right amount of "peacock" in their personality. To be more specific, successful sales people are extraverts, they're very competitive and they have an uncanny ability of knowing exactly when they should, and when they should not "strut their stuff". My favorite business saying is: "Nothing happens until someone sells something". New business development and selling more products and services to existing customers is critical to the success of all companies. So be sure you have at least a few peacocks on your sales team!

Nature

Chameleons are best known for their ability to change color. There are a number of reasons why they do this. Surprisingly "communication" is right up there with "camouflage" as two of the primary reasons. A male chameleon will change colors to attract a female or to warn another male to stay away; but they will blend into the background when they sense the presence of a predator.

Business Lesson

Blending your gestures, tone of voice, how loud you are talking as well as the words you use with a prospect or customer is referred to as mirroring and matching in personal selling. It's an important, effective and easy technique used to establish rapport. By paying attention to the communications style of the person you are talking to and then doing the same thing, I guarantee you will sell more than salespeople who do not practice this technique. Act like a chameleon when you're selling.

Nature

I've never been fly fishing in my life, but I've been told if you aren't using the exact right bait (fly) and if you are not "presenting" it in exactly the right way, the trout won't bite. I also understand that truly great trout fisherman do their homework before they throw their first cast by examining the most recent fly hatch, checking the water temperature and clarity and by paying attention to Mother Nature's biorhythms (solunar tables) to determine the best time of day to fish. If you're fishing for trout … be the trout.

Business Lesson

If you're prospecting for new customers … be the customer. It's a pretty simple concept and it makes a lot of sense, but how many times have you attended a sales or staff meeting where 100% of the agenda was about analyzing your business from the customer's point of view? Typically those meetings tend to focus on internal processes, or issues related to achieving better efficiencies and profitability or better asset management and reducing expenses. What a shame because when it comes to bringing in new customers (and retaining current ones) who will bring in the biggest catch … those who have done their homework and genuinely put themselves into the position of "the customer" or those who haven't?

Nature

Scavengers in Mother Nature have always creeped me out. Whether I'm watching a pack of hyenas gorge on a carcass on the Nature Channel or catching a glimpse of a crow pecking away at some poor flattened critter at the side of the highway, the scavenger part of nature for some reason has never set right with me.

But from what I have read and what I have heard, scavengers are an important and integral component of the natural cycle. I guess nothing is wasted in nature thanks in part to all the scavengers.

Business Lesson

We used to call them "Bottom-Feeders". Whether I was selling industrial chemicals or heading up a mid-sized ad agency, there were companies and sales representatives who seemed to target all the crappy little accounts none of the rest of us were willing to go after. At the time my ego wouldn't allow me to "stoop that low". But looking back on it now, the Bottom-Feeders were pretty darn smart if for no other reason than they had very little competition in obtaining new accounts. I imagine smaller businesses were loyal, as well. All those years a feeding frenzy was happening all around me and I wasn't aware of it.

CHAPTER 10

Branding/Marketing

Nature

The American Indian's concept of the relationship between human beings and the natural world was different from Western Culture. According to American Indian folklore, land simply existed and they merely existed on it. The notion of ownership was foreign to them.

Business Lesson

When it comes to ownership of a brand, the American Indian's philosophy is closest to the truth. As a marketing and advertising professional one of the most difficult concepts I had to explain to clients was the idea that while a company may own its corporate name, its product or its service, it does not own its brand. Yes, I'm aware that when Jaguar sold to Ford it received nearly as much compensation for the Jaguar brand as it was paid for the manufacturing plant and machinery. But my point is that "brand" resides in the prospect and customer's mind and it is created over time through a series of experiences. Brand is the emergent property of everything that is heard, read, said, written or seen and a company does not and cannot own all of that. For more information about branding and managing brand experiences go to the resources section at the back of this book.

Nature

The Platypus is a mammal that lays eggs, has a muzzle like a duck's bill, a tail like a beaver and webbed feet equipped with claws. It's by far Mother Nature's most unique creature.

Business Lesson

No matter what business you are in, one of the most important tasks you'll have is creating your unique, personal brand or as Tom Peters has coined, "the brand called You". Just as the Platypus stands out among all living creatures, in order to be successful you need to differentiate yourself within your department, division, company or within your industry … and the best way of accomplishing that is through branding. The very first step in the branding process is to ask, "What are my core values?" Write out a list of 10 personal values (integrity, creativity, accountability, education, loyalty, honesty, etc.) then cut your list back to the top 3. Think of your core values as the shoulders upon which your personal brand will stand.

Nature

Waves in the ocean are an expression of the ocean. They are connected to the whole ... there is no separation from the whole. While the power of a single wave is amazing, the power of a series of waves is incredible, particularly over time.

Business Lesson

In business every employee is an expression of the organization or of the brand. From the receptionist, to middle managers to everyone sitting in the C-suites ... during an encounter with a customer or prospect, they ARE the company ... they are the embodiment of its corporate values, its mission and its value proposition. What is your company doing to harness this power? What kind of wave power are you generating through your employees?

Nature

Through adaptation and specialization the Giant Anteater has created its own unique niche in the animal kingdom. It has no teeth, sharp claws, a long snout and a tongue that can protrude two feet to lap up the 35,000 ants and termites it will swallow whole each day. No other critter on earth looks, acts or does what an Anteater can do.

Business Lesson

Carving out an area of specialization by addressing the needs of a narrowly defined group of potential customers is referred to as niche marketing. By narrowing your focus you will be better able to serve the needs of your target audience than companies that are trying to be all things to all people. What everyone is looking for in business is "a competitive advantage", and by specializing and capitalizing on your knowledge of your niche market's needs, you will establish yourself as the one and only company that truly understands the customer.

Nature

Kilauea, within Hawaii's Volcanoes National Park, is the most active volcano in the world. It has produced lava that has covered approximately 29,000 acres on the southern side of the island, and built nearly 500 acres of new land out in the ocean. It is estimated that 70% of the surface of Kilauea is younger than 600 years.

Business Lesson

The eruptions and lava fountains in Kilauea are as important to growing the size of the island as a written sales and marketing plan is to growing a small to medium-size business. Less than 40% of the businesses (large and small) my advertising agency worked with had a written sales and marketing plan before we came on the scene. A division of one large company that we worked with increased its sales by 20% over the previous year because the plan that we put together revealed opportunities in the market they never would have detected without the benefit of a formalized planning process. For more information on how to write sales and marketing plans go to the resources section at the back of this book.

Nature

Cardinals fly very differently from all other birds. They swoop up and down in little bursts of energy as if they are surfing sets of waves. There are lots of red birds in nature, but no other species flies like a cardinal – they are truly unique.

Business Lesson

How different is your business from your competitor's business? What is truly unique about your products or services? What sets you apart? Is your value proposition obvious to customers and prospects or does it blend into the market environment? When it comes to strategy, take a lesson from cardinals … and from Michael Porter, Professor at Harvard Business School, "Competitive strategy means deliberately choosing a different set of activities to deliver a unique mix of value. The key is choosing to perform activities differently or to perform different activities than rivals."

Nature

After we introduced ourselves to our Canadian guide his first question was, "What kind of fish do you want to catch?" My youngest son replied for the three of us, "Walleye". "Great, before we shove off let me take a look at your equipment and what's in your tackle boxes – you'd be amazed at the number of guests who come unprepared, or think because they use a particular set-up on the lakes and streams back home, they'll catch fish up here!"

Business Lesson

Sometimes using a marketing or business strategy or tactic that worked well to achieve success at a particular time and place can be reused. But be cautious. As in fishing, conditions change and you're most likely to achieve better results if you modify your approach to match the current situation.

Nature

I was sitting on the beach absorbed in thought when suddenly something clicked in my brain and I became aware of the sound of crickets. The racket they made was so piercing I marveled that I hadn't heard them from the moment I sat down.

Business Lesson

There's an old adage in advertising circles that the moment you become sick of hearing your own advertising message many customers and prospects are hearing it for the very first time. Here's why: the Meritz Dialog Marketing Group estimates that we are exposed to over 3,000 marketing messages per day. So you do the math. If you're running one or two spots per day, what are the chances that anybody will even notice yours? If you're on a small budget you can break through the racket by directing your message to a specific segment of the audience, and by making the spot emotional (100% of ALL buying decisions are affected by our emotions). But crafting and narrowing your message has a fraction of the power of repeating your message time after time after time. So get real about expectations related to responses to your advertising. One or two chances in 3,000! Marvel at the fact that anybody responds to your ads at all!

Nature

Maggots will eat most decaying animal or vegetable matter.

Business Lesson

Maggots have a bad reputation … undeservingly so. They are actually flies that are in the pupa stage of development, and as we all know, flies can facilitate the spread of diseases such as cholera, typhoid fever and diarrhea. However the larva (maggot) in and of itself is actually beneficial to man. In fact, in 2004 the American Food and Drug Administration recognized maggots as a medical device. Use of maggots in medicine is known as biotherapy and it is estimated that one third of the patients who suffer from wounds caused by diabetes could save their fingers and toes if their doctors used maggots for treatment. So what's the business lesson, here? Bad reputations are hard to live down (Exxon is still synonymous with the word Valdez by a majority of people despite the fact that the Prince William Sound oil spill occurred over 20 years ago!). So when it comes to your company and your personal business reputation, guard and cultivate them carefully.

CHAPTER 11

Decision Making Process

Nature

Soil erosion occurs in two ways: Through small events (rainfall or wind-blow) and as a result of large storms. The erosion caused by small common events may appear to be insignificant, but the cumulative impact may, over the long haul, be severe.

Business Lesson

Most of our resources (time, effort and money) at Porter & Associates were spent on big issues or events. Should we buy-out a competitor? Should we open a branch office out of state? Should we resign our largest account? What I have discovered, however, is the impact of all the seemingly small decisions that I made over our 22 year history probably had a more dramatic affect on the company than the larger scale, one-time decisions. To ensure that you are not contributing to the erosion of the values, mission and direction of your company, no matter how small or harmless your decision appears to be ask yourself three questions: (1) Why am I doing what I am doing (what are my deepest personal reasons for making this decision)? (2) What is my intention? (3) What am I trying to achieve?

Nature

During the rutting season male elk choose their battles carefully. Upon encountering another bull they will walk up and down parallel to each other, roaring, bellowing and bugling assessing their opponent's strength and size because they seem to know that even a minor injury could have serious consequences. They rarely square off in head-to-head combat.

Business Lesson

If business leaders took the time necessary to size up a situation like bull elks do during the rut, they would make fewer costly missteps. A classic example of initiating head-to-head combat too quickly was pitting NEW Coke against Pepsi. In April 1985, based upon the results of blind taste tests, the Coca-Cola Company determined that many of their customers preferred the taste of Pepsi. However, if Coke had taken the time to fully analyze and understand its marketing research, they would have discovered that despite their preference for the sweeter taste of Pepsi, customers who drank original Coke were extremely loyal to the brand. So loyal that when the company introduced NEW Coke, Coke drinkers world-wide refused to purchase it and demanded their original formula Coke product back. Luckily the injury Coke suffered that year in the form of customer confusion, discontent and lower sales wasn't fatal to the company.

DECISION MAKING PROCESS

Nature

In the wild, individual animals are vulnerable to predators which is why many species display flocking, schooling and herding behavior … safety in numbers. In an article, "Geometry for the Selfish Herd," evolutionary biologist W.D. Hamilton said each individual group member reduces the danger to itself by moving as close as possible to the center of the fleeing group.

Business Lesson

Herd mentality is common in business particularly during times of uncertainty. Why? Because too many people in business are driven by fear. Obviously, fearful individuals seek safety, and because herd behavior is hardwired into our brains, people in positions of power often times seek safety in numbers. I consider myself to be an expert on this topic because when I was running my ad agency, I made way too many fear-based decisions. Fear is primarily driven by lack of information, so to reduce fear here's what I've learned to do: Gather more data and ask yourself the following two questions, (1) What additional information do I need to move forward with confidence? (2) If I move forward, what is the worst thing that can happen?

Nature

As I walked along the bike path I took notice of a clump of tall weeds to my left. The terrain reminded me of a time that a covey of quail startled me back when I was 11 years old. Playfully I said to myself, "What wild animal lay waiting in those weeds ahead?" And despite my knowing that I was in the "now" and that my quail experience was in the past, I felt my heart race just a smidge as I approached the spot.

Business Lesson

Images, stories and emotions from the past, indeed even those from childhood influence the decisions we as adults are making today. Even those executives who spend a majority of their business day in the left hemisphere of their brain are susceptible to irrational, right-brain creep. Scientists estimate that conscious activity represents only 5 percent of human cognition. Expectations based upon our interpretation of past experiences can create our reality. Are you expecting good things from your subordinates … or bad? Why?

CHAPTER 12

Board of Directors

Nature

The Scorpion and the Frog is a fable about a scorpion that asked a frog to carry him across a river. The frog was afraid of being stung, but the scorpion reassured him that if it stung the frog, the frog would sink and the scorpion would drown as well. The frog then agreed; nevertheless, in mid-river, the scorpion stung him, dooming the two of them. When asked why, the scorpion explained, "I'm a scorpion; it's my nature."

Business Lesson

In March, 2008, Richard Fuld, CEO of Lehman Brothers received a cash bonus of $22 million. Six (6) months later, Lehman Brothers filed for Chapter 11 bankruptcy protection leaving all its shareholders penniless. John Thain, CEO of Merrill Lynch, was named the highest paid CEO among companies in Standard & Poor's 500 Index in 2007 with $83.1 million in salary and bonuses. Nine (9) months later Merrill Lynch was saved from bankruptcy by Bank of America when it purchased all its shares of stock for next to nothing leaving Merrill Lynch shareholders with … well, next to nothing. Scorpions have changed little in the 400 million years since they first climbed from the ocean. So until we find a surefire way to keep them out of top management positions, the best thing we can do to protect shareholders is to place Elf Owls and lizards (scorpion's natural enemies) on the Board of Directors of publically-held companies.

Nature

You can say any foolish thing to a dog, and the dog will give you a look that says, "Wow, you're right! I never would've thought of that!" – Dave Barry.

Business Lesson

Don't surround yourself with people who merely bolster your ego and tell you the things you want to hear. I've seen a few top executives violate this elemental management and leadership rule by appointing an entourage of sycophants to their Board of Directors who helped them maintain their false sense of self-worth, while the company all of them were responsible for governing gradually went to the dogs.

CHAPTER 13

Best Business Practices

Nature

If a Scrub Jay sees another bird watching while it is hiding its food, it will return alone later to hide the food in a new spot to prevent theft by competitors.

Business Lesson

When it comes to protecting confidential and proprietary information, some companies don't have the intelligence of a Scrub Jay! The first line of protecting your trade secrets, customer and vendor lists and other restricted or private information is to have every employee sign a confidentiality agreement. To emphasize that the company is serious about the protection of proprietary information, the agreement should be reviewed face-to-face with new employees. Additionally employees, particularly officers and directors as well as everyone on the sales team, should be required to sign a covenant not to compete. We'd all like to think that all of our employees are honest and ethical so putting systems and processes in place to prevent theft of proprietary information might seem like a waste of time and effort. But trust me; you'll sleep a little better at night knowing that your restricted information is protected from competitors.

Nature

Ticks feed on the blood of rodents, rabbits, birds, deer, dogs and humans. They are major carriers of disease; Lyme's disease is of most concern to humans. To avoid bites, when walking outdoors tuck your pants into boots or socks, tuck your shirt into your pants and apply tick repellent to all your clothing.

Business Lesson

Unfortunately, there are companies "out there" that mimic the blood-sucking behavior of ticks. They bend the rules regarding employee safety, compensation, age laws, worker's insurance, discipline, and equal opportunity. Companies that suck the life's blood out of employees and vendors usually don't have anything in writing related to regulatory compliance or standards of business practice. So to avoid working with these companies, ask one of their sales representatives or an officer of the company for a copy of their employee and/or vendor code of conduct. If the company doesn't have one it doesn't necessarily mean the organization acts like a blood sucking parasite in its interactions with employees and vendors – but just the same, be cautious. And if you haven't developed a document outlining the standards of business practice for your company, get it done! For information and guidance about how to write one, go to the resources section at the back of this book.

Nature

Deer do not overextend themselves. In times of drought and reduced amounts of vegetation, does give birth to fewer fawns and fawn survival rates decline, as well.

Business Lesson

If more people controlled their finances like deer control their population, there wouldn't be as much corruption in American business today. Allow me to explain: Too many people are overextended, financially. Total US consumer debt (installment debt) reached a record level of $2.46 Trillion in June 2007 while mortgage debt reached a record of $10.5 Trillion (Source: Federal Reserve). One in six families with credit cards pays only the minimum due every month (Source: American Bankers Association, Federal Reserve). In short, most consumers are in hock up to their eyeballs, therefore they cannot afford to jeopardize their jobs. This is why many employees look the other way when they encounter illegal or fraudulent business behavior, or refuse to blow the whistle on dishonest supervisors. Hey, its survival of the fittest and if you aren't financially fit, you might do just about anything to protect yourself … maybe even something unethical.

Nature

Squirrels are thrifty – they collect and store nuts so they'll have food throughout the winter. Those that do not store sufficient amounts risk losing their lives.

Business Lesson

Squirreling away money in the form of retained earnings (also called earned surplus, accumulated earnings or unappropriated profit) is the smart thing to do particularly if your business is capital-intensive or if you are in a growth industry. Retained earnings refers to the portion of net income which is retained by the company rather than distributed to shareholders via dividends. Don't make the mistake that I made and distribute most of your company's retained earnings every year. If I had it to do over again I would retain a minimum of 75% of net income each year which would go a long way toward assuring survival during tough times (nearly every business experiences "long, hard winters" at times). And if you own a small to medium-sized business another benefit is retained earnings will have a positive effect on the credit worthiness of your company. Finally, healthy amounts of retained earnings will improve your ability to borrow money based upon the company's financial statements as opposed to providing a personal guarantee.

Nature

Natural disasters are events caused by natural forces that affect humans. They include floods, earthquakes, volcanic eruptions, tsunamis, cyclones, tornadoes, hurricanes and other storms.

Business Lesson

Natural disasters occur in nature and obviously, businesses can be severly impacted by them. Additionally, companies are also exposed to man-made disasters including information security incidents, computer crash and/or malfunction, fire, explosion, ruptured gas mains, air or water contamination, chemical release and a host of other serious incidents that could prohibit a company from continuing normal operations. Despite the fact that these incidents could occur any day, any time, very few organizations have developed a written disaster planning, emergency preparedness or business continuity plan (whichever you choose to call it). Nearly 40% of all small businesses that close due to a disaster never reopen! A well executed business continuity plan could make the difference between success and failure. For more information about how you can develop a plan for your company go to the resources section at the back of this book.

Nature

Red sky at night sailor's delight. Red sky in the morning, sailor's warning. – Well known weather proverb.

Business Lesson

In nature, there are specific "signs" or indicators that can be observed to predict upcoming weather. Similarly, there are key business indicators (KBI) that can be observed to predict the future. One important measurement that many companies fail to include in their KBI is customer loyalty. An article written by Fred Reichheld that appeared in *Harvard Business Review* (2004) suggested companies should measure customer loyalty by asking the following question rather than administering a multi-question survey: "On a scale of zero to 10, how likely is it that you would recommend us to your friends or colleagues?" The difference between the percentage of customers who give high scores (promoters) and those who give low ones (detractors) is referred to as the "net promoter score". A low NPS could indicate that your company is in for some rough weather. For more information about KBI and NPS go to the resources section of this book.

Nature

Dandelions proliferate by dispersing their seeds into wind and air currents where they glide across valleys, plains and mountain slopes far away from the parent plant and colonize free of competition from its own species.

Business Lesson

Biological dispersal, where seeds go in whatever direction the wind is blowing, is a very effective means of propagation for dandelions, but changing your business strategy, business niche or value proposition in reaction to current conditions within your company or industry could be devastating. This occurs primarily because small to medium-sized businesses, in particular, lack a formal planning process. So, if your company has been drifting from one strategic position to another or if its goals and objectives change in the whirling winds of competition, stabilize your situation by developing a written 1-year business plan. For a list of websites you can go to for free planning advice turn to the resources section at the back of this book.

CHAPTER 14

Body-Centered Lessons

Nature

According to Cindy Engel, PhD in Biology and lecturer at Open University in England, wild animals pay close attention to their health. Example: "Up to 90% of the natural diet of wild gorillas consists of the antimicrobial plant Aframomum (a member of the ginger family). What scientists have recently discovered is that this diet cleverly kills pathogenic bacteria such as Shigella and Salmonella while allowing facultative (helpful) bacteria to thrive in the gut."

Business Lesson

Wild animals instinctively recognize the benefits of maintaining a healthy immune system. Unfortunately, most of us in the business world do not, so we skip breakfast, gulp down a cup of coffee and run from meeting to meeting, project to project with an impaired immune system; which of course weakens the body's ability to fend off infection. According to most experts there are three things we can do to protect and strengthen our immune system: improve our diet and nutrition, exercise and reduce stress. I believe a strong immune system starts with eating a well-balanced diet by tapping into what Cindy Engel refers to as our "nutritional wisdom". U.S. businesses lose billions of dollars each year due to absenteeism and reduced productivity due in large part to the secondary effects of poor nutrition. Improving the health of your business may require you to improve the health of your employees.

Nature

All plants and animals possess an internal biological clock. In the 1700s, a French scientist noticed a 24-hour pattern (cycle) in the movement of the leaves of an herb he was studying. The term circadian rhythm was coined many years later.

Business Lesson

Elite athletes and their trainers have been incorporating and exploiting the affects of the human biological clock for many years. There have been many scientific studies verifying a direct link between brain wave activity, hormone production and other biological activities to circadian rhythm. Maybe its time for those of us in the business world to pay attention to the natural rhythm within our body and in so doing maximize our daily output and results. For example, according to the circadian clock in humans, 6:45 am is the sharpest rise in blood pressure; 10:00 am is a point of high alertness while at 5:00 pm people will experience their greatest cardiovascular efficiency and muscle strength for the day (now I know why I prefer to exercise after work rather than before!).

Nature

Here's a little known fact that surprised me - wild animals do active or dynamic stretches before they go into a sprint or leap.

Business Lesson

Ask just about any body worker or chiropractor and they will tell you the most common complaint of today's office worker is persistent muscle stiffness, headaches, and low energy. Nearly all of these symptoms are caused by bad body posture while sitting long hours in front of a computer. The American work place is in need of an injection of active stretching which has been popular in the work places within Japan for many years. Active stretching is different from traditional static stretching in a couple of ways: positions or postures are not held for any duration and the only support that is used is your own muscle strength (no external objects). Active stretching lengthens muscles, loosens ligaments, creates greater flexibility and improves energy flow. To learn more about active stretching and its benefits go to the resources section at the back of this book.

Nature

Some dolphins can hold their breath for up to 30 minutes.

Business Lesson

Holding your breath is basic to survival if you're a dolphin, but if you're a human in the workplace it can be debilitating. Not breathing properly increases stress, increases your heart rate and can negatively impact brain function. The most common situation where people unintentionally fall into the habit of shallow, chest breathing (or, heaven forbid, they flat out hold their breath) is when they are sitting in front of their computer screen, typing. To correct this you need to pay attention to our breath and practice quality breathing. To determine if you are breathing properly, place your hand on your stomach. With each inhale (slowly through the nose) your hand should be pushed out. On each exhale (slowly through the mouth) your hand should move in (toward your body). Simply changing the way you breathe can make a big, big difference not only in your performance but how you feel at work.

Nature

I'm watching two seagulls standing side by side at the water's edge. They're standing as still as still can be, enjoying the mid-day sun and gentle breeze. They almost look like they are napping.

Business Lesson

There was a time when taking a nap was considered a natural part of everyone's day. The desire to nap is a trait shared by many animals. Naps can improve your mood and even your memory. They can revitalize you and the thoughts and dreams you experience may offer you insights about the problems you are trying to solve. We're all trying to be as productive as possible with the time we spend at work, so napping may appear to be counter productive or even an indulgence. But if you'll give it a try, even if it is just a 10 or 20-minute nap, I think you'll feel restored, rejuvenated and ready for the rest of your day.

Nature

In a 3-year study of the reproductive behavior of male black bears conducted by Adrienne Kovach and Roger Powell, encounter rates with breeding females was positively associated with body size (large males fathered 91% of the cubs sampled during the study). Apparently size does matter in nature.

Business Lesson

Size, specifically the height of a male, matters in business success according to Malcolm Gladwell, author of *Blink* (2005). In a study he found that among the CEOs of Fortune 500 companies, 30% were 6'2" or taller (in the general American population, 3.9% of adult men are 6'2" or taller). According to Gladwell, "There is no correlation between height and intelligence, or height and judgment, or height and the ability to motivate and lead people". So the lesson to remember is if you happen to be tall (and male) you have a competitive advantage over your shorter rivals when it comes to advancement within your organization. Thank the members of the genetic pool you come from and go for that promotion you've been after.

CHAPTER 15

Instincts/Intuition

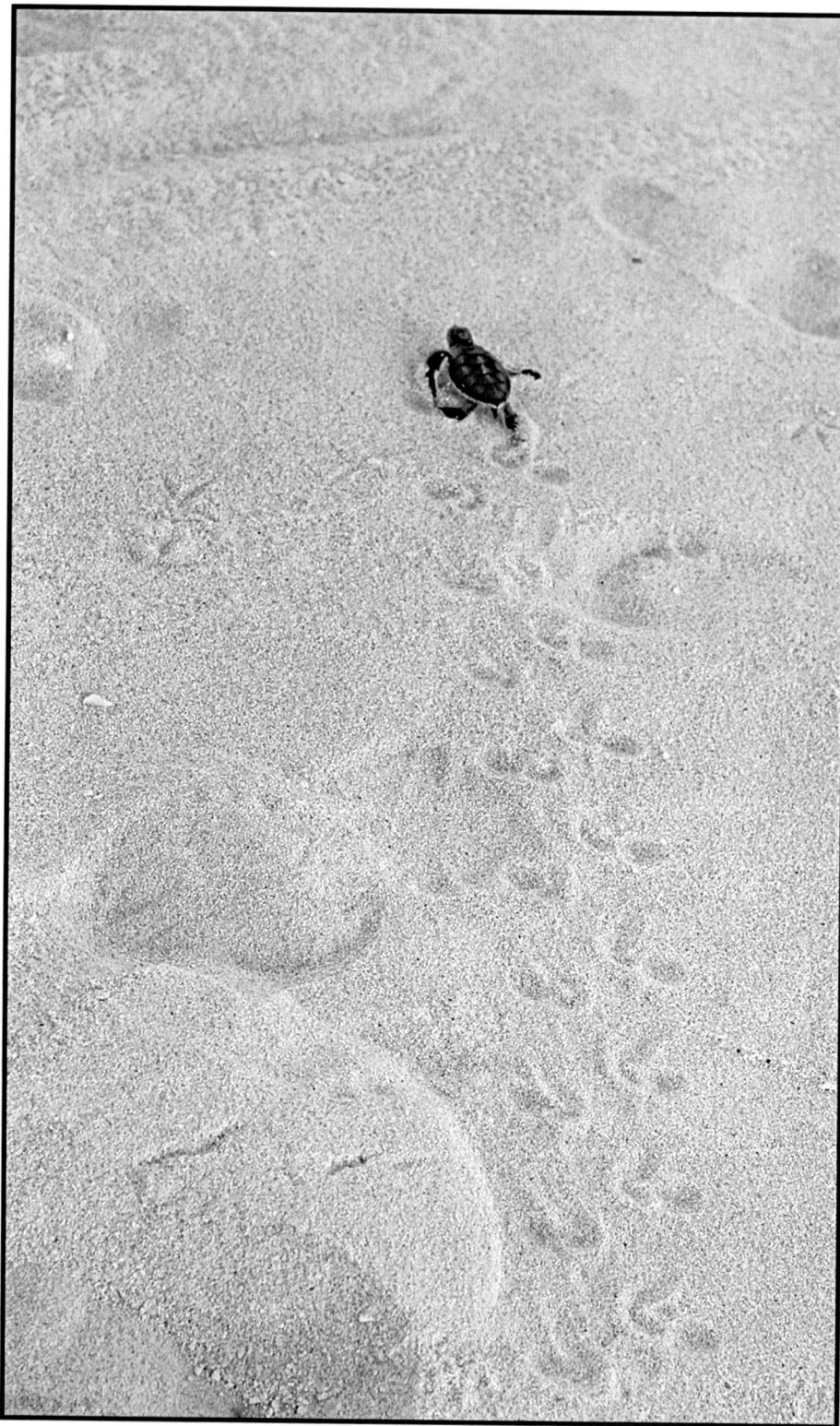

Nature

Newly hatched baby sea turtles don't use MapQuest to find their way to the sea. And even if they could they wouldn't because they were born with something more powerful and much easier to access … their instincts.

Business Lesson

In general most business leaders feel uncomfortable if an individual who reports to them doesn't follow a systematic process of rational thought for a decision or a recommendation they have proposed. However, the most recent research that appears in Malcolm Gladwell's book *Blink* (2005) reveals "truly successful decision making relies on a balance between deliberate and instinctive thinking". So, for better business decisions and better results keep doing what you've been doing but trust your instincts, as well.

Nature

Monarch Butterflies are tough as nails. To look at them with their delicate paper thin wings you wouldn't think they'd have much of a chance at the survival game. To the contrary some groups of Monarch's migrate over 2,000 miles flying from Canada and the United States to winter in the mountains of central Mexico. Looks can be deceiving.

Business Lesson

I hired a guy once who frankly, didn't look like he'd amount to much (he sometimes wore his hair in pigtails!) but for some reason I took a chance and started him off as our ad agency's delivery guy. Seven or eight months after he started, the position as agency receptionist became available, and he cut his hair and won that job over other contenders. Eventually, he became an important resource in our production department, where his ability to facilitate getting jobs done on time and on budget was marveled by everyone on the staff. He's now responsible for millions of dollars of printing at a company known throughout the world for its ability to get jobs done under extreme circumstances. While many HR hiring practices have become highly sophisticated, sometimes it pays to put that information aside and go on your hunch.

Nature

Centipedes never trip! Even with all those legs, their movement is actually very graceful … they almost appear to float. Obviously they don't think about putting one foot in front of the other – they do it by instinct.

Business Lesson

The very first thing most business people do when analyzing a complex problem or a challenge is to break everything down into manageable parts. That process has worked well for many people, but what if someone were to take the centipede's way at the onset by relying on instinct? No truly unique solutions or inventions were derived from the systematic process we call rational thought. Try solving your next problem by getting out of your chair and walking around your office, or your building or (drum roll please) get yourself outside. Suspend your thoughts and be patient … the answer will find its way to you.

CHAPTER 16

Additional Lessons

Nature

In 1948 a Swiss amateur mountaineer and inventor took his dog for a nature hike. When they returned home both were covered with cockleburs. After he dislodged a few from his pants curiosity got the better of George de Mestral. Running to his microscope to inspect one of the burrs he discovered small hooks that enabled the burr to cling to the tiny loops in the fabric of his pants. Within four years he would finish the design and patent VELCRO®!

Business Lesson

Some of the world's most important inventions have been inspired by Mother Nature through a discipline known as biomimicry. According to the Biomimicry Institute, "biomimicry is a new science that studies nature's best ideas and then imitates these designs and processes to solve human problems". Architects, engineers and inventors have been developing manmade imitations of nature's designs since Leonardo de Vinci studied the way birds fly in his attempt to create a flying machine. Modern day examples range from marine engineers who are looking at shark skin for ideas on how to make boats glide through the water more efficiently to researchers at MIT who are copying the water collection system used by a desert beetle. Looking for a break-through idea? Take a hike.

Nature

Remember learning about symbiosis in 9th grade science class? If memory serves me correct, the word literally means "together life" and it refers to organisms that live in close approximation (the truth is I just looked it up at www.marietta.edu, which is Marietta College's website). As a refresher, here's an example of symbiosis provided on the site: White-winged doves have a symbiotic relationship with Saguaro Cactus. The cactus provides food for the bird in the form of fruit … the bird ingests the fruit (and the cactus seeds) … it flies off and later deposits the seeds in another location thereby allowing the parent plant to colonize in new places.

Business Lesson

Back when Kentucky Fried Chicken was in its initial stages of franchising it was rumored that KFC would patiently wait for McDonalds to spend hundreds of thousands of dollars selecting optimal sites for their franchisee. Immediately after the "McDonalds Coming Soon" yard signs went up on a vacant lot, KFC would simply recommend that their franchisee place their business next door. Rumor also had it that in locations where this occurred, sales of both companies were significantly boosted. So you might ask yourself, "How might my company benefit from a symbiotic relationship with one of our vendors … with a customer … or (drum roll please) with a competitor?"

Nature

"There was a time when humanity recognized itself as part of nature, and nature as part of itself. People used images of nature to express this unity and to instill a transpersonal kind of experience." Ted Andrews author of *Animal-Speak* (1998).

Business Lesson

Animal totems are archetypes (primordial symbols) that can help us learn and understand more about ourselves, our companies and our competitors. Here's an idea: The very first book I read on the subject of creativity was Lateral Thinking written by Edward DeBono. One of his creative thinking techniques is to first fully focus on the problem you're trying to solve and then "suspend" all of those thoughts. Secondly, inject the thought of something that is far removed from the problem – the further from the subject the better. This is where visualization of an animal totem might be beneficial. So, for example, you might be trying to solve a marketing distribution problem (suspend that thought) as you visualize an armadillo. Armadillos represent how to use defenses when needed, they protect their vulnerable areas when attacked (real and imagined), and they look awkward. Now ask the questions: How can those attributes help me solve my distribution problem? How might they be getting in the way? I bet you'll come up with new and novel solutions!

Resources

Chapter 1 - Business Philosophy

Steve & Rachel Kaplan have found that the cure for what ails you could be a simple as a walk in the woods - http://www.umich.edu/news/MT/06/Fal06/story.html?awalk

The American Institute of Stress - www.stress.org

Impact of interior plants on human stress & production - http://www.wsu.edu/~lohr/hih/

Into the Deep: Cousteau on the Ocean Crisis - http://www.vistamagonline.com/vista_articles/page.php?tp=0&p=1&id=0&s=into_the_deep_cousteau_on_the_ocean_crisis

Health Hint: Healing Through Forgiveness - http://www.amsa.org/healingthehealer/forgiveness.cfm

The Fringe Benefits of Failure and the Importance of Imagination – 2008 Harvard University Commencement Address - http://www.news.harvard.edu/gazette/2008/06.05/99-rowlingspeech.html

Integral Transformative Practice – What is Leonard Energy Training (LED)? - http://www.itp-international.org/news-events/let-manual.html

The Myth of Multitasking - http://thenewatlantis.com/publications/the-myth-of-multitasking

Be Obsessive About Details - http://www.businessweek.com/smallbiz/content/oct2005/sb20051012_757291.htm

Systems Theory: The Interdependence of All Life - http://paddleasia.com/systems-theory.htm

Determine Your Personal Values - http://www.sustainable-employee-motivation.com/personal-values.html

Chapter 2 - Managing/Supervising/Leadership

About Robert Fritz author of The Path of Least Resistance for Managers - http://www.robertfritz.com/index.php?content=about

Dirty Work, Clean Hands: The Moral Psychology of Indirect Agency - http://www.wjh.harvard.edu/~jgreene/GreeneWJH/Paharia-DirtyWorkCleanHands-OBHDP-09.pdf

Building Character: Strengthening the Heart of Good Leadership by Gene Klann, Center for Creative Leadership - http://www.amazon.com/Building-Character-Strengthening-Leadership-Creative/dp/0787981516/ref=sr_1_1?ie=UTF8&s=books&qid=1243364081&sr=8-1

Global Warming is Accelerating Faster than can be Naturally Repaired - http://www.universetoday.com/2008/04/29/global-warming-is-accelerating-faster-than-can-benaturally-repaired/

Workplace Fear and How To Prevent It - http://www.cio.com/article/476114/Workplace_Fear_and_How_to_Prevent_it?page=1

Teamwork in the Workplace (collection of articles) - http://www.ceoonline.com.au/business/teamwork.shtml

Institute for Ethical Leadership - http://www.ethicalleadership.com/index.html

E-Myth Worldwide - http://www.e-myth.com/

Decision Making Techniques: How to Make Good Decisions - http://www.mindtools.com/pages/main/newMN_TED.htm

Crucial Conversations, Crucial Confrontations - http://www.vitalsmarts.com/

What Is Emotional Intelligence? Definitions, History and Measurements of Emotional Intelligence - http://psychology.about.com/od/personalitydevelopment/a/emotionalintell.htm

Management Not Leadership - http://wildfiremag.com/command/management_not_leadership/?cid=mostpopFC

How to Establish a Mentor Program: Tips for small businesses looking to enhance employee development and performance with formal – or informal – mentoring - http://www.businessweek.com/smallbiz/content/feb2008/sb2008026_636479.htm

Chapter 3 – Corporate Culture

Company Culture: What it is and How to Change it - http://management.about.com/cs/generalmanagement/a/companyculture.htm

Eleven Cultural Values to Run Your Company by … Frank Addante: the Rubicon Project - http://blogs.bnet.com/dogandpony/?p=135

Top 5 Reasons for Leaving a Job as Reported by Employees (2007-2008 Job Satisfaction and Retention Survey) - http://www.onrec.com/newsstories/20698.asp

CEO Mentors: High Performance Culture - http://www.ceomentors.com/mission/hpc.html

What's Empathy Got To Do With It? Bruna Martinuzzi - http://www.1000advices.com/guru/leadership_empathy_bm.html

Chapter 4 – Sustainability/ Ecology

Zero Waste Alliance: Following Nature's Model - http://www.zerowaste.org/

Zero Emissions Research and Initiatives (ZERI) - http://www.zeri.org/

Environmental Waste Solutions - http://www.wasteconsulting.com/

Open Directory Project - http://www.dmoz.org/Business/Environment/Waste_Management/ Solid_Waste/

Solid Waste Solutions Corp. - http://www.wasteaudit.com/dojo/6/v.jsp

Chapter 5 – Control/Change

Small Business Owners Learn How Vision and Flexibility are Win-Win Combo - http:// www.terracycle.net/media/09-05-04--advantagebiz/09-05-04--advantagebiz.html

Think Like a Winner – A Chain Reaction (Brian Tracy in Success March 20, 2008) - http:// www.dreammanifesto.com/thinking-winner-chain-reaction.html

Achieving Market Leadership – Kellogg World Alumni Magazine - http://www.kellogg. northwestern.edu/kwo/sum02/indepth/marketing.htm

Market Leadership Strategies: Winning In the Customer-driven Rapidly Changing Market Place - http://www.1000ventures.com/business_guide/market_leader.html

10 Principles of Change Management: Tool and Techniques to Help Companies Transform Quickly - http://www.strategy-business.com/resilience/rr00006

Chapter 6 – Work-Life Balance

Articles On Work-life Balance: Molly Gordon, Master Certified Coach - http://www.authenticpromo-tion.com/work-life-balance/

Work-life Balance: Ways to Restore Harmony and Reduce Stress (Mayo Clinic Staff) - http://www.mayoclinic.com/health/work-life-balance/WL00056

Alliance for Work-Life Progress - http://www.awlp.org/awlp/home/html/homepage.jsp Wellpower Inc. – http://wellpower.com

Everyday Playtime for Adults: Be a Kid Again (WebMD Feature) - http://www.medicinenet. com/script/main/art.asp?articlekey=51934

Fun and the Importance of Play: Why Adults Need to Play Too - http://stress.about.com/ od/funandgames/qt/play.htm

Chapter 7 – Human Resources

The Myers & Briggs Foundation - http://www.myersbriggs.org/

DiscProfile: Online DISC Profiles & DISC Tests for 35 years - http://www.discprofile.com/

Understanding the Five Element Theory Wood, Fire, Earth, Metal and Water - http://macrobiotics. co.uk/articles/fiveelementstheory.htm

The Five Basic Elements of the Universe: Fire, Earth, Metal, Wood - http://www.1000ventures.com/business_guide/crosscuttings/cultures_5_basic_elements.html

Wisdom Horse® - http://wisdomhorsecoaching.com

Report: Retiring Baby Boomers Expected to Hurt U.S. Companies – Many businesses are not prepared for the loss of experienced workers that will occur over the next decade - http://www.inc.com/news/articles/200703/boomers.html

The Surprising Impact of the Retiring Baby Boomer Generation - http://knowledge.emory.edu/article.cfm?articleid=1184

Marketing Momentum and Tempo: When One Marketing Idea Works It's Time To Strike with Another - http://marketingpr.suite101.com/article.cfm/marketing_momentum_and_tempo

Chapter 8 – Communication

Email Etiquette - http://www.emailreplies.com/

Essential Email Etiquette For Business Professionals - http://www.associatedcontent.com/article/232567/essential_email_etiquette_for_business.html?cat=3

Positive Body Language (Max Wideman) - http://www.maxwideman.com/issacons4/iac1435/index.htm

Top 10 Nonverbal Communication Tips: Improve your nonverbal communication skills with these tips - http://psychology.about.com/od/nonverbalcommunication/tp/nonverbaltips.htm

Nonverbal Communication Skills: The Power of Nonverbal Communication and Body Language - http://www.helpguide.org/mental/eq6_nonverbal_communication.htm

Proxemic Communication - http://changingminds.org/explanations/behaviors/body_language/proxemics.htm

Proxemics: How We Use Space - http://www.bremercommunications.com/Proxemics_How_We_Use_Space.htm

NLP Articles and NLP Strategies - http://www.nlpmind.com/nlp-articles.htm

NLP Articles - http://www.renewal.ca/articles.htm

Communication Barriers - http://www.flatworldknowledge.com/beta-0.1/organizationalbehavior/communication-within-organizat/communication-barriers

Dealing with Workplace Gossip - http://www.management-issues.com/display_page.asp?section=opinion&id=4402

Chapter 9 – Personal Selling

The Four Personality Types - http://www.peppermint-romance.com/Personality-Types.html

Building Rapport a Matter of Eye Contact, Mirroring and Body Language - http://albany.bizjournals.com/albany/stories/2005/02/28/smallb4.html

Reading Body Language for the Sales Professional - http://www.daleygroup.org/css/Articles/

ReadingBodyLanguagefortheSalesProfessional414.pdf

Zappos Lessons: Building a Customer-Focused Culture - http://www.slideshare.net/Thor/zappos-lessons-building-a-customerfocused-culture

Is Your Business Really Customer-Focused? - http://www.surveymethods.com/glossary/article_business_seg_l.aspx

Business Segmentation: Emerging Approaches to More Meaningful Clusters - http://www.marketresearchworld.net/index.php?option=content&task=view&id=1322&Itemid

Chapter 10 – Branding/Marketing

How Legacy Brands Are Reenergized and What Libraries Can Learn from Them - http://www.oclc.org/nextspace/001/1.htm

Working Knowledge for Business Leaders: The Three "Ds" of Customer Experience - http://hbswk.hbs.edu/archive/5075.html

Personal Branding and Career Self-Marketing Tools for Job-Seekers and Career Activists - http://www.quintcareers.com/branding_self-marketing.html

Best Personal Branding Tips: Free Download - http://smallbiztrends.com/2009/05/bestpersonal-branding-tips.html

Motivation in the Workplace: Myths and Tips - http://www.garnetroom.com/id-35/employee_motivation_in_the_workplace__myths_and_tips.html

Employee Motivation: Theory and Practice - http://www.accel-team.com/motivation/

How to Create Employee Loyalty - http://www.net-temps.com/careerdev/crossroads/print.htm?id=1725

First Things First: Create Employee Loyalty to Drive Customer Loyalty - http://ezinearticles.com/?First-Things-First---Create-Employee-Loyalty-to-Drive-Customer-Loyalty&id=1281698

3 Rules for Niche Marketing - http://www.entrepreneur.com/marketing/marketingcolumnistkimtgordon/article49608.html

Write a Marketing Plan - http://www.businesslink.gov.uk/bdotg/action/layer?topicId=1073869186

How to Write a Marketing Plan - http://www.knowthis.com/tutorials/principles-of-marketing/how-to-write-a-marketing-plan.htm

Institute for Strategy and Competitiveness: Michael E Porter Publications - http://www.isc.hbs.edu/

Marketing Strategy: Change Before You Have To - http://ezinearticles.com/?Marketing-Strategy---Change-Before-You-Have-To&id=537392

Why Should I Read Your Ad? - http://www.thomassimmonsagency.com/the_thinking/why_should_i_read.html

The Value of Reputation - http://www.soho.org/Start_Up_Articles/Value_of_Reputation.htm

Social Marketing Journal: Reputation Management the Steve Jobs Way (and other articles) - http://socialmarketingjournal.com/category/reputation-management/

Chapter 11 - Decision Making Process

The Decline of Ethical Behavior in Business: How the Quality Professional Can and Should Meet the Challenge - http://www.qualitydigest.com/magazine/2009/may/article/decline-ethical-behavior-business.html

Respecting Your Business's Ethics Policy: It's Not Enough to Post Your Mission Statement and Values on the Wall. You've Got to Integrate Them Into Your Company's Culture - http://www.entrepreneur.com/humanresources/employeemanagementcolumnistdavidjavitch/article56740.html

The 10 Biggest Blunders (and How You Can Avoid Them) - http://www.businessknowhow.com/manage/businessblunders.htm

Herd Mentality, Herd Behavior: Social Mimicry Among Human Beings - http://knol.google.com/k/peter-greenfinch/herd-mentality-herd-behavior/2m7299842u04v/26?domain=knol.google.com&locale=en#

The Subconscious Mind of the Consumer and How to Reach It - http://hbswk.hbs.edu/item/3246.html

Chapter 12 – Board of Directors

Overview of roles and Responsibilities of Corporate Board of Directors - http://managementhelp.org/boards/brdrspon.htm

The Board of Directors: Responsibility, Role, and Structure - http://beginnersinvest.about.com/cs/a/aa2203a.htm

Free Complete Toolkit for Boards - http://managementhelp.org/boards/boards.htm

Chapter 13 – Best Business Practices

Confidentiality Agreement Form - http://www.morebusiness.com/templates_worksheets/samples/confidentiality.brc

Confidentiality Agreement (sample) - http://www.docstoc.com/docs/6604369/Confidentiality-Agreement-(Sample)

Covenants Not to Compete: A History Lesson and Nine Tips Arising from It - http://www.lawmemo.com/articles/covenants.htm

GAP Inc Code of Vendor Conduct - http://www.gapinc.com/public/documents/code_vendor_conduct.pdf

Baystate Health Vendor Code of Conduct - http://baystatehealth.com/forms/vendor_code_of_conduct.pdf

Southwest Airlines Co. Code of Ethics - http://public.thecorporatelibrary.net/ethics/eth_14186.pdf

Corporate Compliance Insights – Tips for Writing and Updating Your Corporate Code of Conduct - http://www.corporatecomplianceinsights.com/2009/corporate-code-ofconduct-guidelines-policy-tips-writing-updating

Employers Find that it Pays to Provide Financial Education to Employees - http://www.articlesbase.com/finance-articles/employers-find-it-pays-to-provide-financial-educationto-employees-36778.html

Capitalizing Your Company - http://www.smallbusinessadvocate.com/small-businessarticles/capitalizing-your-company-20

Disaster Recovery Planning from A-Z: The Disaster Recovery Guide - http://www.disasterrecovery-guide.com/

Disaster Recovery Template, Business Continuity Planning Booklet - http://www.disasterrecovery.org/index.html

Business Continuity Plan Free Template Download - http://www.ccep.ca/ccepbcp6.html

Would You Recommend Us? That Simple Query to Customers is shaking Up Planning and Executive Pay - http://www.businessweek.com/magazine/content/06_05/b3969090.htm?chan=db

Re-evaluate the Net Promoter Score - http://www.articlesbase.com/marketing-articles/reevaluating-the-net-promoter-score-290614.html

The importance of Key Business Indicators to Small Business Management - http://ezinearticles.com/?The-Importance-of-Key-Business-Performance-Indicators-to-Small-Business-Management&id=1266521

Key Performance Indicators (KPI): How an Organization Defines and Measures Progress

Toward its Goal - http://management.about.com/cs/generalmanagement/a/keyperfindic.htm

Business Planning Papers: Developing a Strategic Plan - http://www.planware.org/strategicplan.htm

500+ Sample business Plans - http://www.bplans.com/

Strategic Planning Resources - http://humanresources.about.com/od/strategicplanning1/
Strategic_Planning_Resources.htm

Chapter 14 – Body-Centered Lessons

Wild Health: Cindy Engel - http://www.wildhealth.co.uk/

The China Study - http://www.thechinastudy.com/

Radical HealthWorks: Proposal for a Workplace Nutrition Education Program - http://radicalhealth-
works.com/nutrition.html

Overview of Circadian Rhythms - http://pubs.niaaa.nih.gov/publications/arh25-2/85-93.
htm

Stretching: The Truth; Basic Neurophysiology Indicates We've Been Going About
Our Stretching All Wrong - http://findarticles.com/p/articles/mi_m0675/is_n4_v8/
ai_9202233/?tag=content;col1

Active Stretching - http://www.one2onenutrition.co.uk/newsletter%20articles/activestretching.
htm

Health Hint: Breathing Exercise - http://www.amsa.org/healingthehealer/breathing.cfm

Breathing – The Proper Technique - http://www.stop-anxiety-attack-symptoms.com/
breathing.html

Waking Up to the Benefits of Napping at Work - http://www.bizjournals.com/columbus/
stories/2002/04/08/editorial3.html

Why You Need to Take a Nap at Work - http://abcnews.go.com/GMA/OnCall/
story?id=2831235

Correlation Between Height and Income No Tall Story - http://www.theaustralian.news.
com.au/story/0,25197,25498079-23289,00.html

The Secret to a Successful Career: Being Tall and Attractive? - http://www.fastcompany.
com/blog/ray-williams/leadership-edge/secret-successful-career-being-tall-andattractive

Chapter 15 – Instincts/Intuition

Basic Instincts: In Business, Sometimes it's Better to Let Your Gut do the Talking - http://
www.entrepreneur.com/magazine/entrepreneur/2007/august/181610.html

How to Make Better Decisions - http://www.forbes.com/2009/02/09/better-decisionmaking-
lifestyle-health_0209_decision_making.html

Gut Almighty - http://www.psychologytoday.com/articles/200704/gut-almighty

Is There a Sixth Sense? - http://www.psychologytoday.com/articles/200007/is-theresixth-sense

(Almost) Everything You Ever Wanted to Know About Creativity - http://www.psychologytoday.com/blog/imagine/200810/almost-everything-you-ever-wanted-know-aboutcreativity

The de Bono Group - http://www.debonogroup.com/

Chapter 16 – Additional Lessons

Biomimicry Institute: Inspiring, Educating and Connecting Biomimics Throughout the World - http://www.biomimicryinstitute.org/

Biomimicry Guild - http://www.biomimicryguild.com/indexguild.html

Symbiosis in Business - http://www.greenseedwebdesign.com/blog/symbiosis-inbusiness/

Employee Swap: Small Company has an Informal Symbiotic Relationship with GE. The Two Companies Trade Employees Frequently - http://www.inc.com/magazine/19891201/6238.html

Start-Up Symbiosis - http://www.forbes.com/2009/06/21/odesk-startups-ebay-technology-internet-venture.html

Animal Totem - http://www.animaltotem.com/

Books of Interest

Biomimicry: Innovation Inspired by Nature by Janine Benyus (2002) - Biomimicry is the science and art of emulating Nature's best biological ideas to solve human problems. Non-toxic adhesives inspired by geckos, energy efficient buildings inspired by termite mounds, and resistance-free antibiotics inspired by red seaweed are examples of bio-mimicry happening today. Benyus says, "The more our world functions like the natural world, the more likely we are to endure on this home that is ours, but not ours alone."

Blink: The Power of Thinking Without Thinking by Malcolm Gladwell (2007) – A book about the choices that seem to be made in an instant – in the blink of an eye – that actually aren't as simple as they seem. How do our brains really work? And why are the best decisions often those that are impossible to explain to others? Blink changes the way you understand every decision you make.

Buckminster Fuller's Universe: His Life and Work by Lloyd Sieden and Lloyd Steven Sieden (2000) – A biographical study of one of the great minds of the 20th century. Sieden succeeds in demonstrating how his search for Nature's underlying rules of harmony and efficiency is relevant to fields ranging from aviation and manufacturing technology to environmentalism, housing, parapsychology and extraterrestrial anthropology. (From Publishers Weekly)

Cannibals with Forks by John Elkington (1998) - demonstrates how all businesses can and must pick up the three-pronged fork of sustainability to help society achieve the interlinked goals of economic prosperity, environmental protection, and social equity.

Cool Companies: How the Best Businesses Boost Profits and Productivity by Cutting Greenhouse Gas Emissions by Joseph Romm, Island Press (1999) - shows how energy efficiency investments improve productivity, yield high return on investment, and mitigate climate change. Another important book about the next industrial revolution which is accelerating Earth toward a better tomorrow.

Cradle to Cradle: Remaking the Way We Make Things, by William McDonough & Michael Braungart (2002), North Point Press. The authors propose replacing "reduce, reuse, recycle" with "Waste equals food". The former perpetuates the cradle to grave mentality that still creates enormous waste. Products can be designed to mimic nature and provide nutrients that can be assimilated by the earth.

Crucial Conversations: Tools for Talking when Stakes are High by Kerry Patterson, Joseph Grenny, Ron McMillan & Al Switzler (2002) – A breakthrough book. You'll learn how to: Prepare for high-stakes situations with a proven technique; transform anger and hurt feelings into powerful dialogue; make it safe to talk about almost anything; be persuasive not abrasive. You'll never have to worry about another conversation again.

The Discipline of Market Leaders: Choose Your Customers, Narrow Your Focus, Dominate Your Market by Michael Treacy & Fred Wiersema (1997) – This is a book about the discipline needed to attain and sustain market leadership. It's based on five years of research and practice conducted with CSC Index, the fastest-growing management consulting firm in the world. The central theme is that no company can succeed today by trying to be all things to all people. It must instead find the unique value that it alone can deliver to a chosen market. Many practical guidelines and examples from wellknown companies help make this a must read book for all business men and women.

In Earth's Company by Carl Frankel (1998) - Identifies the key elements of the emerging era of corporate environmentalism and details the many concepts and technologies for creating a sustainable future that have already been developed and are in place.

The Ecology of Commerce: A Declaration of Sustainability by Paul Hawken (1994) - Hawken is on a one-man crusade to reform our economic system by demanding that First World businesses reduce their consumption of energy and resources by 80 percent in the next 50 years. He believes that "we need a design for business that will ensure that the industrial world as it is presently constituted ceases and is replaced with human-centered enterprises that are sustainable producers." This book is full of captivating ideas.

The First 90 Days: Critical Success Strategies for New Leaders at All Levels by Michael Watkins (2003) – A road map for taking charge quickly and effectively during critical career transition periods, whether you're a first-time manager or a new CEO. Watkins outlines proven strategies that will dramatically shorten the time it takes to reach what he calls the "breakeven point": the point at which your organization needs you as much as you need the job.

The Green Revolution: The American Environmental Movement, 1962-1992 by Kirkpatrick Sale (1993) - A 108-page history of the Green or environmental movement in America from 1962-1992. Chapters include origins, sixties seedtime, 1962-70, doomsday decade, 1970-1980, the Reagan reaction, 1980-1988, endangered earth, 1988-1992, and prospects.

Hope, Human and Wild: True Stories of living lightly on the earth by Bill McKibben (1995). Inspiring stories about sustainable communities such as Curitiba, Brazil and Kerala, India.

How Customers Think: Essential Insights Into the Mind of the Market by Gerald Zaltman (2003) – Zaltman argues that 95 percent of thinking happens in our unconscious. Therefore, unearthing your customers' desires requires you to understand the "mind of the market," that dynamic interplay between the consumers' and the marketers' thoughts that determines the outcome of every buying decision. He offers rich insights into what happens within the complex system of mind, brain, body and society as consumers contemplate their needs and evaluate products.

The Last Hours of Ancient Sunlight by Thom Hartmann (1999). The author proposes that the only lasting solution to the crises we face is to relearn the lessons of our ancient ancestors--who lived sustainably for thousands of generations. When you touch this new yet ancient way of seeing the world and hearing the voice of all life, you discover that you, personally, hold the power of personal and planetary transformation. In that breathtaking moment, we see both a possible future for the survival of humanity and the fulfillment of our highest dreams and aspirations.

Earth in the Balance: Ecology and the Human Spirit by Albert Gore Jr. (1992) – Former Vice President Gore demonstrates that the quality of air, water, and soil is at grave risk, not only locally or regionally but globally, and argues that only a radical rethinking of the human relationship with nature can save the earth's ecology for future generations.

The Growth Illusion by Richard Douthwaite (1999 Revised Edition) - Reveals in a compelling argument why economic growth has enriched the few, impoverished the many, and endangered the planet. "Growth in fact produces jobs in exactly the way a chain letter produces money," says Douthwaite on page 87. An enlightening and honest appraisal of the effects of pursuing economic growth.

Introduction to Forestry Economics by Peter H. Pearse (1990) – Peter Pearse is Professor Emeritus at the University of British Columbia and a specialist in natural resources management and policy. Dr. Pearse has conducted several public inquiries on natural resources in Canada. He has been awarded the Forestry Achievement Award, the Distinguished Forester Award, the Order of Canada, and the Jubilee Medal.

Mapping the Journey: Case Studies in Strategy and Action toward Sustainable Development by Lorinda Rowledge, Russell Barton and Kevin Brady (1999) - Case studies which provide visions of a more sustainable future, and shed light on the path, milestones and solutions -- in particular the management processes these organizations employed.

Materials Matter: Toward a Sustainable Materials Policy by Kenneth Geiser & Barry Commoner (2001) - Lucid text on the state of materials use, design, and production. Geiser demonstrates the unsustainability of current materials practice, the use of toxics, and the production of waste. He argues for the need of a sustainable materials policy while also outlining how the design of sustainable materials would remove toxics from the environment and reduce the amount of waste entering into the environment.

Mid-Course Correction, Toward a Sustainable Enterprise: The Interface Model by Ray Anderson (1998) - Jim Hunt, Governor of North Carolina, says this book "combines bottomline business sense with a passionate desire to leave tomorrow's children a healthier planet. The result is a blueprint for corporate environmental responsibility that should be required reading in every board room and business school."

Natural Capitalism by Paul Hawken, Amory Lovins, and Hunter Lovins (1999). A new business model is outlined in the much-praised book. Exerts and chapters can be down-loaded free using Adobe Acrobat Reader from the Natural Capitalism website at www. naturalcapitalism.com. This book is a 'must read' for leaders in government and business.

The Natural Step for Business: Wealth, Ecology & the Evolutionary Corporation (Conscientious Commerce) by Brian Nattrass & Mary Altomare (1999) - This book examines how four very successful "evolutionary" corporations in Sweden and the United States - including IKEA and Scandic Hotels in Sweden, and Collins Pine and Interface in the U.S. - are positioning themselves for long-term competitiveness using The Natural Step as a central part of their corporate strategy. Nattrass and Altomare puncture the myth that a company must choose between profitability and care for the natural environment, and present a timely and practical application of this exciting model for global sustainability.

The Path of Least Resistance for Managers by Robert Fritz & Peter M Senge (1999) – You will learn why organizational structure may impede organizational learning, that achievement in one part of an organization may not be replicated because of organizational barriers. You will be introduced to key principles of structural tension and structural conflict, examples that demonstrate why best efforts do not always result in success, and suggestions on ways to redesign organizations so that they can succeed.

Plan B: Rescuing a Planet under Stress and a Civilization in Trouble by Lester R. Brown (2003) – Focusing on the food sector, Brown predicts a food crisis in which China will soon begin competing with U.S. consumers for U.S. grain. He proposes Plan B – a worldwide mobilization to stabilize population and climate and to raise water productivity by half.

Ripples from the Zambeszi by Ernesto Siroli (1999) - Empowers and inspires communities anywhere to develop the ability to create their own prosperous future in the face of the forces of globalization.

The Sacred Balance by David Suzuki and Amanda McConnell (1997) - Is highly recommended for an explanation of humanity's place in nature and our utter dependence on its gifts of air, water, soil and the energy of the sun.

The Sustainability Advantage: Seven Business Case Benefits of a Triple Bottom Line(Conscientious Commerce) by Bob Willard (2002) - Former IBM Senior Manager makes the first systematic quantification of the business case for including environmental stewardship in bottom line thinking.

The Tipping Point: How Little Things Can Make a Big Difference by Malcolm Gladwell (2000) - A wonderful book on how an idea, trend, or social behavior crosses a threshold, tips, and spreads like wildfire.

Upsizing, The Road to Zero Emissions: More Jobs, More Income and No Pollution by Gunter Pauli (1998) - Considered by some to be a utopian target, zero emissions as a concept clearly describes what business and industry of the future must aim to achieve.

Many of the books (and book descriptions) listed here were reproduced from the Zero Waste Alliance website: www.zerowaste.org

Index

About the Author

Tom Porter is an entrepreneur and recognized authority on branding, marketing and advertising. He was the president and CEO of one of the Midwest's most respected marketing communications agencies which he sold 22 years after founding the company. Clients were local, regional and national advertisers including John Deere, Brunswick, Meredith Corporation, Disney and the U.S. Senior Golf Open.

Always an outdoor enthusiast and former marathon runner he enjoys whitewater rafting, bicycling, fishing and long-distance walking. He subscribes to the notion that American business ethics are currently at an all-time low. Porter hopes that in some small way the principles and lessons that have created abundance in the natural world for billions of years will be utilized inthe business world to help reset our moral standards and create new possibilities for how we run and grow our organizations.

For more information about the book, please visit:
www.businesslessonsfromnature.com

Author's photography by Lila Stafford.

NOTES

LaVergne, TN USA
22 December 2009
167927LV00003B/1/P